Reflections of

Tara Gandhi Bhattacharjee
1934 to Mahatma Gandhi's youngest son Devadas Gandhi and Lakshmi Devadas Gandhi. Her husband Dr. Jyoti Prasad Bhattacharjee was a well-known economist. She has two children: a daughter, Sukanya Bharat Ram and son, Vinayak Bhattacharjee. Tara has dedicated her life to working for the betterment of Gandhi Smriti and Darshan Samiti. She has been working for many years for the uplift of rural women, children and society with the Kasturba Gandhi National Memorial Trust set up by Mahatma Gandhi.

Reflections of an Extraordinary Era

TARA GANDHI BHATTACHARJEE

With a foreword by
Vinayak Bhattacharjee

Translated from the Hindi by
Maneesha Taneja

HarperCollins *Publishers* India
a joint venture with

New Delhi

First published in India in 2012 by
HarperCollins *Publishers* India
a joint venture with
The India Today Group

First published in India in Hindi as *Asadharan Yug Ke Sadharan Din* in 2009
Original copyright © Tara Gandhi Bhattacharjee 2009
Foreword copyright © Vinayak Bhattacharjee 2012
English translation © Maneesha Taneja 2012

Photographs courtesy Tara Gandhi Bhattacharjee, Vinayak Bhattacharjee

ISBN: 978-93-5029-232-7

2 4 6 8 10 9 7 5 3 1

HarperCollins *Publishers*
A-53, Sector 57, Noida, Uttar Pradesh 201301, India
77-85 Fulham Palace Road, London W6 8JB, United Kingdom
Hazelton Lanes, 55 Avenue Road, Suite 2900, Toronto, Ontario M5R 3L2
and 1995 Markham Road, Scarborough, Ontario M1B 5M8, Canada
25 Ryde Road, Pymble, Sydney, NSW 2073, Australia
31 View Road, Glenfield, Auckland 10, New Zealand
10 East 53rd Street, New York NY 10022, USA

Typeset in Charter 10.5/14
by Jojy Philip

Printed and bound at
Thomson Press (India) Ltd.

Dedicated to Amma and Appa

MAP OF DELHI FROM THE 1940s

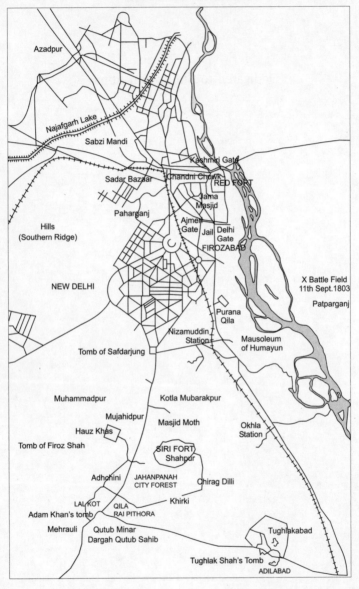

MAP OF INDIA FROM THE LATE 1940s AFTER PARTITION

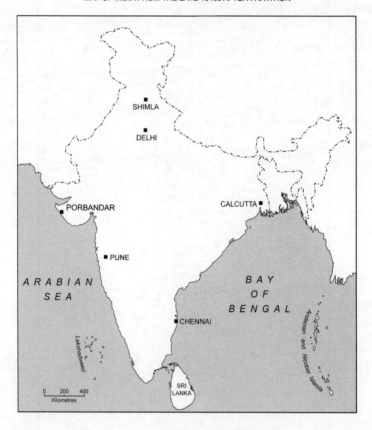

MAP OF CENTRAL AND NORTH DELHI FROM THE 1940s

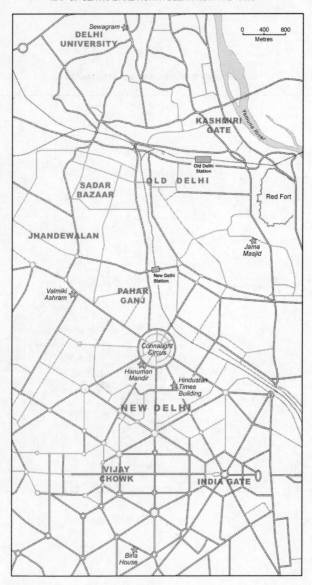

MAP OF DELHI AS IT IS TODAY

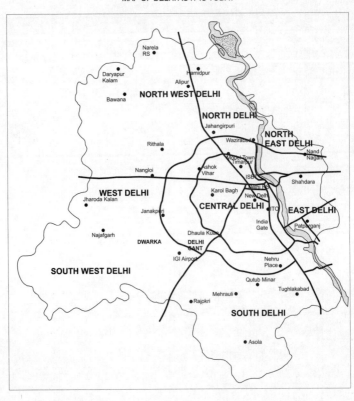

Contents

A Son's Foreword

❧

This is a book about the experiences of a young girl during an extraordinary and tumultuous period in recent Indian and world history. The seventy-eight-year-old lady recounting her childhood memories is my mother, Tara Bhattacharjee, born Tara Gandhi and known to me, my sister Sukanya and countless others simply as Ma.

Ma was born in Delhi on 24 April 1934, the eldest child of Devadas and Lakshmi who subsequently also had three sons: Rajmohan, Ramchandra and Gopalkrishna. As a granddaughter of Mohandas Karamchand (Mahatma) Gandhi and of Chakravarti Rajagopalachari (popularly known as Rajaji), her early experiences from the late 1930s and '40s are a virtual moving image of that era, a real period piece. In 1911, the capital city of colonial India moved from Calcutta to New Delhi, and landmark buildings like the colonnaded circular Connaught Place and the art deco Viceroy's residence were completed in the 1930s. This book dwells on what Delhi was like at the time, and, since it is written retrospectively, it highlights how Ma has been a witness to the transformation of Delhi into the metropolis it is today.

The recollections also beautifully capture the mood of the period and reflect on thoughts, sensations and philosophies that can be drawn from moments of deep change and intense human interaction. The pages speak for themselves and I am far from being an impartial observer. My main purpose in writing this introduction is to set a context to help the reader approach the stories related by Ma with sympathy and warmth. Within this book lie some of the events and experiences that shaped Ma's personality. This, coupled with my intense interest in India, have compelled me to commission this translation of the Hindi original published several years ago. Through this faithful English translation, I hope to share my mother's insights with a broader audience and with her many friends across the world. So, while there are dollops of selfish interest in seeing this book through, I do believe that in Ma's storytelling lie some beautiful reflections on humanity, spirituality, the character of legendary leaders, and the nature of the Indian society, which is the result of incredible cultural mixing over the last 5,000 years.

India is not often held up as a role model nation and heaven only knows how much needs to be fixed in the country. It would take a treatise to list down and analyze the multitude of problems in this country, but at the core the issue today is a carelessness that has crept into its society – carelessness in the execution of public services. And this carelessness is tolerance taken too far. The point I am making is that India is no longer a poverty-stricken country and has had a very long spell of economic growth that has created a wealthy and worldly middle class. It is certainly incumbent on these middle and wealthy classes, if not on everyone, to not accept poor levels of public service. Nor should they act as if it is outside their gift to make a difference for the society at large.

Freedom of press and an independent judiciary have helped in generating some change though. Over the past year or so, the nation has seemed to shed its complacence on some issues such as the decades of corruption that has made billionaires of many public officials. More generally, consider that as we gaze at the Arab Spring, the Euro crisis, the modern wars of imperialism and wonder what of Pax Americana, we should spare a thought for a country that is today one country, one currency zone, has 22 official languages with as many scripts, is arguably the most culturally and racially mixed society in the world, has sprung and/or provides shelter to countless philosophies of life (Hindu, Buddhist, Sikh, Jain, Zoroastrian, to name a few) and houses the world's three Semitic religions. It is also the world's biggest democracy.

Most of the world's nations are tribal in nature in the sense that many of their citizens are bound together by some or all of a series of common traits: racial background, language, politics, religion, to name a few obvious ones. Such tribalism is a source of strength to those that it binds, but we should not forget that it is equally good at excluding and ostracizing those from other cultures and with other bonds. It is important to be conscious of this simple reality as we now live in an increasingly globalized and interconnected world. In the book by the BBC production, *The Story of India*, Michael Wood retold a quote from an Indian journalist that encapsulates one of India's real strengths – its diversity:

'...when Sonia Gandhi, widow of Rajiv Gandhi, Nehru's grandson...stood down as PM-in-waiting after the 2004 election, you saw the unlikely situation of an Italian Catholic woman as prime minister-elect giving way to a Sikh who

swore the (prime ministerial) oath to a Muslim president
in a majority Hindu nation. Now, I ask you, where else on
Earth could that happen?'

And now to return to Ma's book. Amongst the many
people Ma recalls and mentions in the book are her
paternal grandfather, Mohandas Karamchand Gandhi, her
father Devadas, her mother Lakshmi and her maternal
grandfather Rajaji. Her sense of amazement in looking
back is evident as these memories are of her parents,
grandparents, family and friends and not of the same people
as leaders, statesmen and visionaries. These are memories
of individuals about whom claims were later made such
as – 'Generations to come will scarcely believe that such a
one as this walked the earth in flesh and blood' – as Albert
Einstein said of Mahatma Gandhi upon his death.

Ma displays a subtle bewilderment in recounting her
stories as the events and people she describes have since
fundamentally shaped humanity at least in the Indian
subcontinent for over half a century. The experiences
themselves are wonderful examples of a child's impressions
of things, and in their recounting they are unfettered by
the passing of time. In that sense, they are no different
from the memories of countless other children. The power
of hindsight is what makes them extraordinary.

To not beat around the bush, my mother is unusual. Not
in any eccentric way but in the way she leads her life and
embodies with unconscious ease many contradictions in
the context of today's societies. Thus, she is a strong mother
figure while never having played the traditional role of a
mother; a successful and impactful leader of organizations
without ever having worked in corporate environments, let
alone studying business administration; a spiritual friend,

philosopher and guide to many people, although a rebel at heart; a craver for attention who is at her happiest on her own.

Ma is currently the Vice Chairman of Gandhi Smriti and Darshan Samiti, India's leading memorial to Mahatma Gandhi and the site of his martyrdom. She is an accomplished and highly-regarded social worker who has worked with women and children in the villages of India through the Kasturba Gandhi National Memorial Trust (an institution founded by Mahatma Gandhi) of which she is a trustee. While a major supporter of women's welfare, she has famously shunned the activist slogan of 'female awakening', and instead, maintains that it is not for women but for men to awaken, known as 'purush jaagaran' in Hindi. In a similar vein, she maintains that it is the mothers who are to blame for the continuity of male domination in Indian families because they do not raise their daughters and sons with the same values; they are not taught alike and are given different tools with which to tackle life. Ma's impartiality is refreshing in a society that has constitutionally sponsored affirmative action in many areas of life, with all the benefits and pitfalls that this brings. As an example of her experiences in this field, we have included in this book some essays by her. These talk about women as victims in conflict areas, the Gandhian philosophy of *Khadi,* and about her passion for dolls.

Ma maintains that she has found a meaning in life through her work with the spinners and weavers of *Khadi,* a cloth that is entirely handmade, from the spinning of the thread to the weaving of the fabric. She draws a symbolic parallel between hand-spinning and the proverbial thread of creation linking man with his origins. As a recognition of her efforts in this cottage industry, she was appointed a member on the government's *Khadi* and Village Industries board, a position she held for several years.

Ma is a gifted linguist, fluent in Hindi, Bengali, Urdu, Italian, and of course, English, while being conversational in Gujarati, Tamil, Punjabi and French. A couple of years ago, she informed me that she would have to give up her lessons in Mandarin as it was impinging too much on her time and that she had reached the limits of her ability to usefully absorb more languages. Needless to say, I didn't even know that she had started taking these lessons.

She has not aged mentally and instead her natural inquisitiveness is perhaps more acute today than all those years ago as a mother of two young children. Recently, already in her mid-seventies, she remarked to me that number 9 was a magic number. 'How do you mean?' I asked, puzzled. 'Whenever you add it to another number between 1 and 9 and add up all the resulting digits, the original other number is returned,' she replied factually. Any number theorists out there will not be surprised and will know well the many notable properties of 9 in our base 10 number system. Instead, what is remarkable is that having consistently failed maths at school and university and fearful of the subject all her life, she now approaches the subject with curiosity and precision and has independently identified a mathematical perplexity! She doesn't look at it in this way, of course, and for her this is just a beautiful discovery at which to marvel.

One day while travelling with her in a car in Delhi, I observed that she was holding biscuits and other small snacks in her hand. Normally cars stuck in Delhi traffic are besieged by children, women and men displaying all types of ailments and demanding charity. But it was different that day as no one appeared and after the long wait at yet another traffic signal, she sighed to me, 'You see when one is prepared to give to a beggar, then try as hard as you might, none will appear. They only appear when one is least able or willing to satisfy their asking. One should try to give when one is least able; it is not giving if you give only on your own terms.'

There are a hundred more stories I could recount that would fill a whole book, and I do not want to be guilty of writing only through rose-tinted spectacles. My sister and I alone know the challenges of interacting with a single parent who is headstrong, driven and charismatic. Often I feel that she is the child and we the elders, occasional role reversals occurring since my father's passing. In fact, the hardest thing about our relationship is accepting the life choices of the other and in having the other accept help from you. Despite all its strains and challenges, my sister and I have always had an extremely close relationship with our mother, and we consider ourselves fortunate for the depth and trust of our three-way bond.

My mother has had three distinct periods in her life: childhood, married life, and life after fifty and as a widow. Through these phases, she grew from being an extremely privileged though rebellious child to a pampered middle-aged lady with her erudite diplomat husband and children in Rome, and finally to a single woman beyond her fifties leading a tough, challenging and ultimately rewarding life.

This book is about Ma's childhood and her family. As the eldest of four children, she had responsibility thrust upon her from an early age. Her fondness and caring for her brothers has been ceaseless, a love reciprocated by the brothers and their families. Each brother has achieved enormous success in his respective field in addition to being an internationally accomplished writer. More recently, and particularly after my father's passing, her brother Ramchandra was a deep inspiration to her. As one of the most gifted Hindu philosophers of our time and as a man who practised what he preached, Ramchandra Gandhi was a well-known figure in India and in the international academic circles who sadly passed away in 2007.

At the core of my mother's spirituality and humanity are two key figures: her mother and her husband; in other words, my grandmother and my father. You will hear more about my grandmother in the memoirs that follow, and hence I will limit myself to a few paragraphs on my father whose own background is symbolic of and intertwined with the phenomenal evolution of Indian society.

Jyoti Prasad (or 'Baba' as I called him) was born in 1922 when the British empire, financially burdened by years of imperialist expansion and the debilitating effects of World War I, began to steadily unwind. He was born in the village of Bhatpara, District 24 Parganas North, outside Calcutta in today's West Bengal. The address, still current today, is yet another remnant of the infrastructure left to India by the British, in this case of an organized postal system and its associated administrative order.

As a son of the leading Brahmin family of the village, Baba was born into respectability and responsibility, and went on to achieve recognition and success as an economist, initially in rural Bengal at Tagore's Viswabharati University in Shantiniketan,then later in the Indian government in New Delhi, and finally at the United Nations in Rome, Italy.

Twelve years younger than him, my mother met my father at Shantiniketan in the mid-1950s, and later, they married – the result of love and not arrangement. This was unique for the time, and even more so, given their different Hindu castes. My mother's statesmanlike family was no reason for my father's family to compromise on fundamental Hindu principles; they maintained that no Bhattacharjee family member would attend the wedding in Delhi. My father's father, Dadu, did bless the union as he was very fond of his youngest son and equally of young Tara, but not without substantial debate via written correspondence between him and Rajaji, himself a Brahmin who had blessed the wedding of his own daughter, Lakshmi, with a lower caste banya – Devadas – the son of Mahatma Gandhi. Thus, Tara's wedding took place in March 1957 and was held at 1 York Place (currently, 10 Janpath), which subsequently became the residence of Lal Bahadur Shastri, who in 1964 succeeded Nehru to become India's second prime minister. Dadu did eventually yield and allowed a few distant relatives to attend what was to become the society wedding of the year.

Bengal's role in India today is somewhat diluted, but back in the '30s and '40s, it was the very backbone of cultural India. It was the seat of reformist and progressive movements. Writers such as Tagore, painters such as Jamini Roy, and the rich tradition of theatre and folk music in Bengal helped to strengthen the confidence in Indians to stand on their own and demand independence from Britain. For most Indians of the time, Bengalis were the period's equivalent of the Renaissance Tuscans, and thus despite the wedding 'snub', Ma's family felt honoured to have a distinguished Bengali son-in-law.

Bhatpara is the mainspring of the Bengali Bhattacharjee clan, and an epic saga could be recounted about this village and the clan. How it has evolved in the shadows of economic and migratory cycles, our ancestral home there, the family itself and in particular Jyoti's father, his elder brother Sambhu and Sambhu's wife who is alive today – all put together make for a potential Satyajit Ray movie. Bhatpara is also the home of progressive India where an inter-caste wedding was allowed at a time when no one other than a Brahmin was allowed into the kitchen for fear of staining the purity of the house. This marriage was indubitably about love even if it must have been sparked by Tara's rebellious streak.

As is so often portrayed in Indian culture and mythology, great achievement comes through great sacrifice. And so goes the legend of Sambhu who sacrificed his lifestyle to help secure his younger brother's future. When Baba was offered a scholarship to study for a PhD at the University of Illinois, Dadu forbade him from going as leaving the shores of India was considered blasphemous at that time. Until this point, Sambhu had led a socially active life as the extrovert son of a well-to-do Brahmin businessman. As the cardinal unit of the village, the family needed worthy sons who could run the business, act with leadership in the community and play the many ritualistic roles expected of a clan head, including that of leading communal *pujas* at the family temple situated within the main house complex. Sambhu's love for his younger brother steered him to take responsibility for all this so that Baba could be free to pursue academics and a career outside Bhatpara.

Dadu passed away in 1959. By then, he had seen the return of my father, his prodigal son, after six uninterrupted years in the United States, and had embraced Tara as a daughter-in-law and blessed the birth of Tara and Jyoti's daughter, my older sister Sukanya.

Sambhu's wife, Santvana, eighty-five years old and alive today, is a living representation of traditional Bengal. She is my Bodo Ma (or elder Ma) and is a paragon of Bengali simplicity and sophistication, attired almost always in simple white saris. She is herself a Bhattacharjee from Bhatpara and is one of nine siblings. To the best of my knowledge, she has not been outside Bengal very often, and has left Bhatpara only a few times in her life to go to Calcutta, or on pilgrimages to sacred sites in India. Today she is a diminutive figure, bent over after decades of sitting on the ground cooking for the family on a coal stove. Her mind is sharp and her voice brilliant as ever. She grasps things fast and is never surprised by world events, technological revolutions or global cultural idiosyncrasies, a trait that can at best be explained by the self-confidence that comes from being truly grounded in her own immediate society, a society which views itself as at the pinnacle of knowledge and teaching. She is above it all and has seen all manners of human interaction and socio-economic change from the window of her Bhatpara kitchen. She is the bearer of tradition and could have been Ma's greatest detractor, but instead she always showered Ma with love and praise, as she does to this day. This is significant because she, more than any male in the house, has upheld the household rituals around purity; under a lesser woman's watch, Ma would not have been allowed into the first floor of the house, let alone its kitchen.

The Bhatpara home stands unchanged by time, its yellow Italianate façade the same as I recall from the days

I spent there as a child with Ma, Baba and Sukanya. In the hot monsoon months of July and August, we would spend a few weeks in Bhatpara eating Bengali food cooked on charcoal stoves and passing lazy afternoons resting by the tall windows overlooking the family temple. Dinner would not start before 10 p.m. and the evenings would merge into late nights *addas* with my cousins, aunts, uncles and parents. Things change slowly in Bhatpara; it was only in the mid-1980s that a dining table was introduced into the house, and a fridge arrived a few years after that.

Baba returned from America in the mid-1950s and established a centre for agricultural research at the university of Shantiniketan in West Bengal. From there he went on to distinguish himself as one of the great planners of the Indian socialist system and, together with other notable agricultural economists, as one of the minds behind the Green Revolution. His success in this field led him to a career with the United Nations, which in the mid-1960s took him to the headquarters of the Food and Agricultural Organization at Rome in Italy. This was the era of the Italian 'miracolo' and of the late 'dolce vita'. This is where my sister and I spent our childhood, and during our twenty-year sojourn in that eternal city, Ma was primarily a mother, a wife and a homemaker. It certainly feels today that it was an idyllic childhood, and, unlike many others in the diplomatic communities, we integrated with the local Italian community effortlessly. We learnt the language, cooked the food, toured the country, and cultivated many local friends.

Baba died suddenly in 1986, and Ma, Sukanya and I relocated to Delhi during that summer. While our links with Italy still remain strong today, Ma has gone a step ahead and metamorphozed her relationship with the country from a domestic one to a working one. Given her affinity with the country and her fluency in the language, her life experiences and philosophies have attracted great interest in Italy where she is a frequent panellist and guest of honour at many conferences on peace, science and environment. The combination of Ma's spiritualism with the flair and creativity of Italian enterprise has produced many beautiful and unique outcomes. You will find an example of this in the photo section of the book where the Italian telecommunication company, Telecom Italia, has used Gandhi's imagery to heighten the significance of modern means of communication.

The romantic period of our family life in Rome came to an abrupt end with Baba's passing in 1986, marking a clear watershed into Ma's next stage in life – the current one. In some senses, this is the most accomplished phase of her life, but it has been characterized by struggle and search. Ma had a break point at the age of fifty and she literally had to reinvent herself after her husband's death. Her children had left home to build their own careers and destinies, and she found herself completely alone. She was forced to find a new purpose in life. She rediscovered her independent spirit, and that, coupled with a strong resolve, led her to spirituality and social work. In a recent video interview covering the publication of a friend's book on women's lives after deep change, Ma said that her loneliness led her to look at life differently, and to consider everyone as her family, to dispel differences amongst people and, instead, be one with all.

When asked about Gandhi and her relationship with him, my mother often says that she is a granddaughter of

Mohandas Karamchand Gandhi, but not a descendant of Mahatma Gandhi. The truth as I see it, however, is that over the past twenty-five years, her ambitions combined with her search for spiritual insight and balance has made Ma lead her life in many ways like him. Not in any ascetic way as one might do by wearing only white and by shunning jewellery. While she wears only the *khadi* material, she enjoys fashion, bright colours and silver jewellery, and takes pride in her appearance and looks. Nor has she consciously imitated Bapu to achieve spiritual enlightenment.

Instead, the challenges she has faced, coupled with her own character, have led her to gravitate towards many of the qualities that defined Mahatma Gandhi: conviction, perseverance, honesty, truthfulness and leadership. Living these qualities comes with its own share of daily struggles, which she endures by relying mainly on her copious reserves of stubbornness.

Ma has always been a contemporary person, a woman of the times who has enjoyed fashion, music, food and entertainment. Today she lives in her eclectically decorated house, surrounded by her hand-made dolls, supporting staff and their families, her own family and friends while dealing with the vagaries of modern life in Delhi. She does not lead an austere life nor does she impose her way of life on others. She does have a motto in her life – she is doing it 'her way' as in the classic Sinatra song. She is unusual and has accomplished the unusual.

She is now searching for her connection with the eternal and spiritual. Just a few months ago, she remarked that she is now struggling to find a motivation in this life. I was profoundly saddened by this comment, but on reflection I realized otherwise. Hinduism believes in unity between creatures and the creator and, that life on earth allows us to experience an existence apart from the universe and the universal spirit. Eventually they come back together and this temporary duality returns to a singularity. The Sanskrit term for this is *advaita*, which simply means non (*a*) duality (*dvaita*). This then gives rise to a beautiful and deeply philosophical definition of love, namely the coming together of the physical and the spiritual in one energy form.

Hindu philosophy postulates that humans may experience some or all of the four stages (*ashrams*) in their lives on earth: *Brahmacharya, Grihastha, Vanaprastha* and *Sanyas*. The first ashram is about learning, avoiding material wealth and ostentation, building physical and mental discipline to prepare for the second ashram. In *Grihastha*, you seek the pleasures of life. You become a father or mother and are active in family life. You are an active and giving member of society. In the third stage, you seek detachment from physical possessions and greater bonding with a broader community than your immediate family and friends. You have experienced prosperity and family life, and can rightfully claim material possessions, but you do not seek them. Physical detachment from a social and material life is your objective. This process is long and tortuous, and leads to search and introspection. This road leads you eventually to *Sanyas*, and in this fourth ashram, you finally give up physical possessions and ordinary life. What remains with you is the search for spiritual unity, namely *advaita*.

While there is a sequence to these stages, it is recognized that they do not necessarily appear for everyone in this logical sequence. Nor is it expected that everyone will experience all the stages. Ma spent a long time in *Grihastha* as a result of her pampered childhood and married life. Over the past twenty-five years, she has been in *Vanaprastha*, and has enjoyed being part of a large global family of friends. Most recently – and perhaps this is the reason for her comment that she has no motivation in life, she has entered the detached phase of *Vanaprastha*. This is a difficult phase. It requires deep introspection and a conscious separation from possessions and social relationships acquired and nourished in *Grihastha* and early *Vanaprastha*. While the path ahead is difficult, Ma's objective is pure, and there is nothing to be sad about that.

Enjoy the book.

October 2012   Vinayak Bhattacharjee
London

Harijan Ashram

⌘

My first conscious memory is of what is known as Kingsway Camp in north Delhi. Almost seventy-five years ago, situated at one end of Delhi, in the sprawling village centre was an ashram called Harijan Colony. In that ashram we had a lovely, small house. The first few years of my life are strongly imprinted on my consciousness for their simplicity.

Those were extraordinary days marked by a nation's fight for independence, and my father had to deal with the challenges that journalism offered in such exciting times. Precisely for that reason we left the ashram at Harijan Colony and shifted to the Hindustan Times Apartments in Connaught Circus. I clearly remember our luggage being packed in our small house. It was probably morning. I can still recall the clean smell of freshly laundered clothes – mine and those of my siblings. Our hearts too were filled with freshness. Outside, the sun shone brightly. In just a while we were to leave for our new home. We children were eager to go to our new home, though there was a certain sadness at leaving the familiar surroundings.

Despite the eager anticipation of change, my young heart felt apprehensive about losing the simple life of Harijan Colony. Would my childhood be left behind here forever? These thoughts ran through my mind like wildfire.

My childhood and the village environs were left behind, but my earliest recollections are still about the simple village life we had then.

Though we children were excited about the new beginning in the huge flat in Connaught Place, in some corner of our hearts we yearned for the open skies and earthy smell of Harijan Colony.

I ran into the new flat with my brothers, holding a doll in my arms. 'Ma, where shall I put my doll to sleep?' I asked mother.

'Not here. This is the drawing room.' Ma explained in Hindi but using the English term 'drawing room'.

I ran to my brothers and told them, 'You know, there is a big room for drawing here.'

Mother explained to me that a drawing room was indeed the sitting room.

Connaught Place in those days was very different from the Connaught Place of today. In 1940–41, the clear night sky was filled with shining stars. Standing on the terrace of our Hindustan Times Apartments we brothers and sisters would peer down at the road. Before dusk fell, men would climb up the poles on the roadside and light up the street lamps. The lamps probably ran on gas. Seeing those men climb up and down those poles every evening was a big source of entertainment for us. In the summers, men with huge skin bags would sprinkle water on the road. There were very few people. There was a lot less chaos as well. There were no three-wheelers and very few scooters, if at all. Also, there were few buses on the road. Today's traffic is beyond the farthest margins of our imagination. Tongas and horse carriages were the general mode of conveyance then. The horse carriage today is a reminder of the hassle-free times of a bygone era.

But my childlike mind was also witness to the cruel reality of this mode of conveyance. The sound of the whip being used on horses tied to the carriages carried over to us on the second floor and would disturb and sadden me greatly. I felt a silent pain surge within me. Man's cruelty to animal and society's acceptance of this cruelty was my introduction to the harsh reality of life.

The beauty of truth also strongly influences a child's consciousness. The smell of wet earth, the sight of those lamps lighting up one by one – even after all these years, these memories are vivid in my mind.

I have an unforgettable incident to narrate from that time. Like all little girls, I was also very fond of dolls. Below our flat were the newspaper office and the press. A carpenter used to work there. Father used to praise the carpenter, Nanhe Mian, a lot. One day I went to him with my doll. I almost ordered, 'Nanhe Mian, please make a swing for my doll.'

'Sure. I will.' Saying this, he collected some pieces of wood, and before you knew it, he had put together a beautiful swing. His sincerity and dedication are forever etched on my mind. Today, I see Nanhe Mian as a sculptor carving a statue. For the wish of a young girl, the sculptor put in all his ability, creativity and dedication. It is also possible that through his art Nanhe Mian also tried to express his gratitude towards my father. Children capture all nuances. In the hammering of those pieces of wood, my little heart could hear the carpenter's inner thoughts. It was like a dream come true when that little swing was ready and I picked it up with both my hands.

'You won't get it today, little girl. I will varnish it and give it to you tomorrow,' Nanhe Mian said, smiling. In his voice, there was the excitement of seeing to completion a job well done. And in those words of the dedicated craftsman was also an advice to be patient.

My love of dolls outlasted my adolescence and youth, and persists even today in old age. My lifelong association with dolls and its stories always begin with the memory of Nanhe Mian. You may wonder how I remember the incidents of my childhood and youth with such clarity. Even my mother used to be amazed at my memory. But this natural power that I have is not extraordinary. Some people talk of their lives at the age of one and two! Some memories of the long gone past, of people, and the ambience of times gone by are still intact in my memory.

A few decades later, I was invited to a programme to felicitate Shri Viyogi Hari-ji in the ashram at Harijan Colony. I stood in front of our old home. Delhi had changed. Even that extension of Delhi was no longer rural. But that old house was just the same as it had been aeons ago when we had lived there. It was as if I had been transported back in time. I was the protagonist as well as the viewer.

I did not go inside. It was somebody else's house now. I had no desire to find out how many families had made their home there. Those moments of the past, difficult to describe, frozen in time, are clear as crystal. The rural, pollution-free air of that era, the smells of cows, buffaloes, cow dung, wood stoves and raw earth had me in their spell. Then suddenly I remembered that there used to be a jungle in front of the house. I turned around to look, but the forest was no longer there. Then I looked in front of me. The house stood there, the same as before.

All of us children would go off into the jungle to play. Mother would stop us. We never went too far into the forest, but it would scare Mother nevertheless. It was difficult for her to understand the attraction nature has for children – how we longed to play in the lap of nature with full abandon. Once, when we came home after playing, I found Mother waiting for us – nervous, worried and worked up. 'Listen, don't go into the jungle to play, and if you hear a man laughing, don't go investigating.'

'Whose laughter? Which man?' I asked.

'It's not a man.' Mother explained. 'It's a hyena who laughs like a man. Children get taken in by the sound and go near it. The hyena lures little children and catches them.'

I can never forget how frightening those words were.

We used to come home covered in mud, and had to be cleaned up innumerable times a day. Just changing our clothes and keeping us clean would tire out mother so much. And when Dada and Dadi came to visit us, looking after them and attending to guests who came to meet them, while looking after us, must have been exhausting for Mother. Today I can only imagine how tiring it must have been for her. But the presence of my grandparents brought so much cheer that every day seemed like a festival. Bapu-ji would stay in our house at Harijan Ashram. Sometimes Ba would come and stay there alone, without Bapu-ji. We children would jump for joy on hearing the news of her arrival. There was a heavenly purity in the smell of sandalwood and sunshine that was an integral part of her body and her *khadi* sari with a coloured border.

Decades later, that day, as I stood before the house, all those memories from the past came flooding back to me. Mother's voice, Dadi's perfumed presence, the company of our cousins, Father's busy life, his head shaking with worry (which did not leave my child's mind untouched). Gandhi's independence movement was at its peak. Independence was the unknown factor. Satyagrah was the known factor. Dada, Dadi, Nana, Tau, Kaka, Mama and all their companions were constantly in jail. Father would be jailed on and off for publishing news of the Satyagrah. Amidst all this, Mother and Father remained focused on our upbringing.

In our small house, we did not have a fresh-water tap and we probably didn't have electricity either. But there was definitely a traditional luxury. Today when I think about it, it seems to be totally feudal in nature in the context of Gandhian philosophy. In one of the rooms, there hung from the roof a *khadi* curtain, which was one-fifth the height of the walls. On one corner of the curtain was a rope that hung to the ground. On moving the rope up and down, the curtain worked as a fan. As far as I can remember, this comfort had turned into a plaything for us children. I vaguely recollect a young boy, who was employed to help in the house, swaying the curtain-fan. I also vaguely remember that Father thought of it as a necessary evil. Perhaps he had installed the fan for Ba's comfort; in his desire to serve Ba, he could pull that rope all night. The fan must have been there for Mother's comfort as well, because mother suffered from illnesses like pneumonia and pleurisy in those years. Today such fans seem to have become a symbol of our cultural heritage, out on display at exhibitions.

Made and run by hand, this useful apparatus was a symbol of our exploitative society – a society for whose upliftment Mahatma Gandhi worked so hard. Anyway, it is true that even sixty-four years after Independence today, we haven't taken any concrete steps for the rehabilitation of the downtrodden. The cord of the fan has in its various forms tied us down.

I remember Mother working hard all the time. She would take care of all the kitchen chores. If I can't quite visualize my mother squatting on a low stool in front of a wood stove, it is not because my memory has faded; it must surely be the smoke from the stove that makes the picture hazy.

I once told mother, 'You would do a lot of work in the Harijan Ashram.'

Mother said, 'I was young then. I could easily manage the sweeping, mopping, washing the clothes, doing the dishes.' Her burden would increase because of visitors. 'I used to get upset only because having guests meant less time for kids,' she added.

'But yes,' Mother reminisced, 'when I used to fall ill, Bapu-ji would send Ba to look after you children. Ba would never stay away very long from Bapu-ji, but she wouldn't leave you kids until I recovered completely. Neither did you leave her alone for a minute.' Recently I found a letter written by Bapu-ji to Mother. In that short note, written in 1935, Bapu-ji tells Mother that if Tara is very ill, Ba is willing to go and look after her.

That day in front of that house, Mother's words echoed in my thoughts. I always saw Mother being a good hostess in the best Indian tradition. Despite all the responsibilities, she always had time for us.

In the ashram there was a round temple in front of the house. That day my eyes automatically sought out the temple. Its creation is part of my first conscious memory. A painter from Gujarat came to adorn the walls of this temple when it was built. He told my brother Mohan and me very affectionately that he needed our help with the painting. 'I will draw and paint on the walls from atop a stool or steps. You please hold my colour palette. I can then bend and take the colours I need.' We were thrilled at the idea. Father was happy too. Mohan and I would stand there helping the painter. We used to call him Bhatt-ji. The entire ashram was excited about the construction of the temple. Bapu-ji was to come for its inauguration. Assisting Bhatt-ji was an extraordinary experience for us. Children feel rewarded when entrusted a responsibility with affection and trust, and that experience becomes a warm memory as they grow up. Children are very intuitive. People's natural considerations touch them in a way that they never forget.

The temple was complete. I don't remember the day of the inauguration. Recently I came across an old photograph in which Bapu-ji has a small girl in his lap wrapped up in a sheet and there is another younger child sitting next to him. I think the picture is from the inauguration of the temple.

Leaving behind the rural ambience of the ashram, I naturally took with myself, in my memory, some people and families. Annaro, a village girl who used to help mother in and around the house; Mangal Bhai, the carpenter in the ashram; and a teacher's family of Indian Tamil origin from Malaysia – none of us can ever forget these people. Annaro had a rustic charm, Mangal Bhai was friendly, and the Malaysian family was rather modern for the times. These loving people were my first introduction to society outside of family, and I believe one's first experience of the world outside home shapes one's personality. In my seventh decade today, I understand that these people, my first friends in the world outside home, were extraordinary in their ordinariness.

Even after leaving the ashram, we used to nag our parents to take us back every week to meet these old friends. As soon as we reached the ashram, Mangal Bhai would come running to meet us. He would say, 'Tara, Mohan, you still come to visit us, but gradually you will stop coming. Don't forget us.' Mangal Bhai's words, along with our own displacement, had a strong effect on our minds. Till many years later, I continued comparing every place to life in the ashram.

So, yes, coming back to the point, I was rooted to the spot in front of our old house in the Harijan Colony, caught in a moment from memory, overcome with old sounds and smells. Standing there I saw Kasturba. I could clearly hear her words: 'Wash your hands and eat. Oh my God, your clothes are so...' The dream broke. I was looking at my clothes. They were probably not as clean as Ba would have liked them to be. And yes, I was hungry. And then another reality broke my bubble. From behind me came a voice changing the rhythm of my internal music: 'Let's go, Tara. The meeting is about to start.' There was a meeting in the ashram in memory of the Late Hari-ji.

These days I constantly feel a strange curiosity, a strange excitement. I am searching for the unknown supreme power in the absolute beauty of the known powers of a mother.

Sewagram

Ba would come and stay with us in the Connaught Place flat, but Bapu-ji never managed. For Bapu-ji to stay anywhere, it was essential to organize a place for public gatherings. After coming to the Hindustan Times flat from the ashram, I would picture Ba and Bapu-ji in Sewagram, Bardoli Ashram and in the Aga Khan prison. My memories of the Bardoli Ashram are very blurry. In the Sewagram Ashram, we lived in a mud hut. In the night, we would sleep outside under a clear sky. With the first rays of the sun, Bapu-ji would come smiling to wake us up. The place always smelled of the *Harsingar* (Nyctanthes flowers). There were many coral trees in the ashram and sweet-smelling flowers covered the ground beneath the trees. Mother used to pick those flowers. She would explain to us that just before the first rays of the sun appeared, these flowers would by themselves fall off the trees and we were thus saved the violence of plucking them from the branches. She would tell us that we could even take these flowers for Bapu-ji because they were procured non-violently and were fit for an offering to him. She would pick the flowers while we would enjoy a morning walk with Bapu-ji.

In Sewagram, everyone would eat together, sitting on the floor in a line. Before the meal, a small Sanskrit *shloka* was chanted. Constantly hungry from all the running and playing in the open environs of the ashram, that short prayer seemed rather long to me. The food in the ashram tasted incredible. It is today that I understand well that prayer. It has a beautiful meaning: May He (God) protect us. May He use us. May both of us (Master-disciple) be vigorous. May we never become enemies. Om. Shanti. Shanti. Shanti.

The open clear skies of Sewagram, the smell of the earth, the village hut, the touch of pure *khadi*, Bapu-ji's enchanting personality, a morning walk with him, and then the *Harsingar* flowers – I see these memories weaving an endless yarn on the *chakra* of time.

Aga Khan Palace

❧

Ba and Bapu-ji were imprisoned in a wing of Aga Khan Palace in Pune along with some of their companions. My siblings and I would go there with our parents to meet them; we went there with as much enthusiasm as we would go to meet them at the railway station or in Sevagram Ashram. We would be so impatient to meet our grandparents that the journey from Delhi to Pune seemed endless. In Pune, we would stay in a two-room inn near the station. Mother would cook for us in a small kitchenette (probably for the lack of proper arrangement of food at the inn), and then we would be off to the Aga Khan Palace in a tonga. Before entering the palace, permission had to be sought from an English officer for the visit. Father would go to the officer's house to seek permission. This entailed a long wait for us in the tonga outside, but Father never came back without the permit. Ba and Bapu-ji would be so thrilled to see us that the sombre atmosphere there would be instantly dispelled.

❧

A ten-year-old girl lay quietly with her grandmother on a cot. She had come with her parents and younger brothers to meet her grandparents. Even though she had been suffering from a long illness and was extremely weak, the grandmother's sari, her sheets and pillows were redolent of love and that special feeling that was unique to her and made the granddaughter feel secure. Every touch was familiar, but why was there a note of farewell in her grandmother's voice? It's amazing how children can always tell.

There was no anguish in her farewell; just an acceptance of nature's decision. 'Why is Dadi looking at me thus?' thought the child. 'Is she going to leave us? How will I live without her love?' The grandmother's feeble hands caressed the girl's head with a tenderness she knew too well.

The child looked at the grandmother, wanting to say a thousand things. But she was always deterred by her Dadi's peaceful smile and expressive eyes. She gave the little girl a beautiful white *khadi* sari with exquisite embroidery on the border. This was the first sari she ever had. 'This sari is for you,' the grandmother told her. The child had never been so happy. She held the sari as if it were a handful of flowers. She could not believe that the sari was hers to keep. She clung to it for dear life and turned to her grandfather with a question in her eyes. Would he let her take the sari? Dada always gave away everything to the needy.

The child's eyes were questioning her grandfather. Would he ask her to give this sari to somebody else? He understood what she was trying to say. He smiled and she got her answer in his smile: 'This sari is yours.' Maybe the child was the needy one that day – needy of her grandmother's love.

∞

Bapu-ji would lightly talk about his routine and the rules of his house arrest. I was always curious about the hall adjacent to the area where Ba and Bapu-ji had been kept. The doors to the hall were always open. 'The doors are open anyway, so why can't we go in?' I asked Ba.

'Whether the doors are open or shut, we are not allowed to and we shouldn't go in there,' Ba gently explained to me. Today, I understand the meaning of those words said by Ba in confinement that day; the meaning of self-rule or 'swaraj' is 'self-control'.

Even while under house arrest, Ba would always have treats ready for us. Bapu-ji would stick to his routine even then: prayers at three in the morning, spinning yarn, reading, meditation, writing etc., a controlled diet, exercise, and then evening prayers. Everything was just as it used to be at the ashram.

For us, Bapu-ji and his smile were inseparable. It was in Aga Khan Palace, during Ba's long illness, that I first saw Bapu-ji without a smile on his face. He seemed like a stranger. And that is how we knew that the situation was grim.

It was in Aga Khan Palace that Mahadev Desai passed away in 1942 after a serious illness. It must have been a hard blow for Gandhi and Kasturba and must have taken a lot of their spiritual strength to accept the death of their secretary who was like a son to them. Coupled with this, a lifelong Satyagrah, worrying about fellow Satyagrahis, the prevailing air of unrest in the country, a prolonged illness, and the thought of her husband being alone after her death must have been quite unbearable for Ba. Her children and all their companions were devoted to her. Dr. Susheela Nayyar and her brother, Pyarebil Nayyar, had dedicated their lives to the service of Ba and Bapu-ji on the express wishes of their mother. Ba had full faith that Bapu-ji would be very well looked after by her family, and even more so, by their companions. Nonetheless, Ba found it unimaginable to think of being separated from Bapu-ji. Ba had been incarcerated in different jails many times, but in the Aga Khan Palace, her last incarceration, she dearly missed the huts of Sevagram.

The English were talking of releasing Kasturba because of the seriousness of her illness, but more to save face. Kasturba turned down the offer without batting an eyelid, saying that as long as as other women freedom fighters were in jail, she did not wish to be freed, for real freedom was in India's independence. Physically, she did not live to see India's moment of independence, but history and time were her witnesses. Freedom fighters and countrymen mourned her death alike. Statesmen and foreign dignitaries offered their condolences and cited her role in Gandhi's journey.

I have always been inspired by how Bapu maintained his ascetic lifestyle, even in jail. Prayers, meditation, reading, writing, spinning, etc. would start at three in the morning. Most of the writings by the great freedom fighters were done in jail. Given his thirst for knowledge, Bapu-ji would always manage to learn one new language. He used to also practise writing with his left hand. According to psychiatrists and health experts today, right-handed people should practise writing with their left hand and vice-versa. Such a practice helps us fight many diseases associated with old age.

Even in the sombre atmosphere of the jail house, Bapu-ji's sense of humour and optimism filled the ten-year-old girl – me – with joy. I still clearly remember Bapu-ji's unbridled laughter when he told my father that the British government had covered the window of his room with a black cloth so that people wouldn't be able to see him from outside.

In the limited time allotted to us to meet him, Bapu-ji would put aside his spinning as well as his writing. In jest, but also with the aim to teach us, he would always ask, 'Do you practise letter writing? Has your handwriting improved? You must learn Tamil from your mother.' I don't remember if we could write to them in jail. But I do remember that Bapu-ji always stressed on the art of letter writing. In that era, the postcard was an important part of life. Today, a postcard could be considered impolite. But I am looking at its importance during Gandhi's times from a different perspective. It was cheaper than paper and envelope. The quality of paper used in a postcard was always better. And because of its size, only what was important was written. It also saved time. Since it was an open document, nothing remained a secret – neither the writer's language nor thoughts.

Bapu-ji would take us to the garden in the jail house. The presence of a badminton court in the garden was a source of endless enthusiasm to Bapu-ji. Once, he actually wanted to play with us, but couldn't do so due to lack of time.

On a wooden cot in the veranda, Ba lay confined to the bed due to a long debilitating illness. Along with the Gandhian principles of truth and *ahimsa*, I was also strongly moved by the anguish that was part of Gandhi and Kasturba's life. Today, sixty years later, I look at their anguish from another perspective.

We are talking of an era before the advent of computers,

the Internet and cell phones. In the confines of the Aga Khan Palace, since Gandhi was denied access to radio, telephone and newspapers, no contact was possible with the outside world. Innumerable men and women were incarcerated along with eminent leaders of the freedom movement. There was no way to discern what the British government was thinking or doing. 'Where is everyone? How is everyone?' Thoughts like these about his friends and confidants must have constantly plagued Gandhi. But a man's mind cannot be confined by the mere walls of a jail; it is free. Meditation and a firm belief in truth were what gave him strength and defined the goals of truth and *ahimsa*.

Even a young girl like me understood the anguish hidden behind Bapu-ji's smile. With the limited intelligence of a ten-year-old, I was trying to fathom the reason for his anguish. Today, six decades later, I can see Kasturba's life flit past in my imagination, and can finally comprehend Mahatma Gandhi's anguish.

In my thoughts is a fourteen-year-old girl. According to the custom then, fourteen-year-old Kastur was married off to Mohandas Karamchand Gandhi of the same age in 1882 in Porbandar, Gujarat. Both the groom and the bride belonged to well-to-do trader families of Kathiawad, Porbandar. Kastur was a young girl brought up and steeped in the customs, traditions and the lifestyle of Kathiawad. Unaware of household responsibilities, a girl's world is all about dolls and toys. In the natural course of life governed by customs and traditions, girls like Kastur leave behind their parents, families and dolls to accept a new life behind the veil. This is not a thing of the past. This is a reality even today in certain sections of our society.

I can visualize shackles of custom holding a fourteen-year-old girl prisoner behind a veil and stifling her carefree spirit. But the question is whether that girl, in the full bloom of her life – in the jangling of her bangles and the tinkling of her anklets – had any clue about the direction in which her life was headed. Did she have any inkling about the extraordinary path her life was to take? In the long afternoons in her new home or when the sun had set, sometimes waiting and sometimes in the beloved's arms, what wordless sound touched the young girl's heart that foretold of an unknown life far from the routine of a normal existence. I don't know if Kasturba ever spoke to anyone about these experiences. In the responsibilities of daily life and societal pressures, she may herself have been unaware of these feelings. It is true that I am only imagining Kastur's early experiences of married life. I am neither a poet nor a historian that I can do justice to Kastur's fascinating life experiences.

The many historical and important films that have been made on Gandhi also feature Kasturba. Attenborough has shown the last few decades of Gandhi's life, and Shyam Benegal has made an excellent film on Gandhi's Satyagrah in South Africa. These films have played and will continue to play an important role in spreading Gandhi's message.

Gandhi's childhood, youth and his life in Porbandar have not yet inspired any filmmaker to explore these as potential subjects for a film. This facet of Gandhi's life can be explored through Kastur's life as well. Kastur's life in the context of the ambience, culture and society of Porbandar in those times would pose a challenge for any filmmaker. Kastur was 'Kasturba' before Gandhi became the 'Father of the Nation'. I now search for Kastur's identity in Kasturba.

In her last days in the Khan Palace, how did Gandhi see her – as Kastur or Kasturba? I wonder.

This question will always remain unanswered. It is not based on any proven fact. It is the result of my vivid imagination.

At the same time, I don't wish to give any impression that may be contrary to the truth that was Gandhi. It is also an undeniable fact that Gandhi's thoughts, work and other aspects of his life will always remain worthy of research. Gandhi in Kasturba's context and Kasturba in Gandhi's will also be studied deeply.

In the end, in Gandhi and Kasturba's life, truth and non-violence are what remain supreme.

Shimla

∞

My brothers and I met Bapu-ji in 1945 in Shimla after his incarceration in the Aga Khan Palace came to an end. But the general mood there was so light that my eleven-year-old mind did not comprehend Bapu-ji's loss of his lifelong companion. Father knew that Bapu-ji would be in Shimla during our summer vacations and took us along with him. My youngest brother was born that very year in April. Amma and Appa reached Shimla with Mohan, Ramu, a month-old Gopu and me. There was a cluster of two to three houses atop a hill. Ma set up house for us in a bungalow called Carlton Grove. My maternal aunt and uncle also came there as did my paternal cousin Sumi. The kitchen was well stocked, we had good beds to sleep on, and there was ample space to play inside as well as outside the house. I was, of course, incapable of taking in the vastness of the arrangements that had to be made. And it must be for this reason that I have no recollection about how mother managed all the arrangements so well, while taking care of us and a month-old child. Households then were very different from those today. I have vague

Bapu and Kasturba

Bapu and Kasturba

Kasturba with Gokul Das (Bapu's sister's son), Harilal, Manilal, and Ramdas

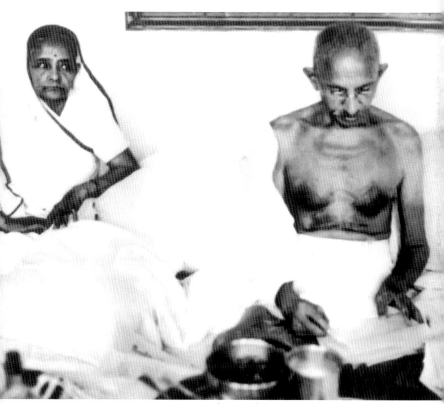

Bapu and Kasturba

Bapu and Kasturba

Bapu's return from South Africa, 1914

Bapu with son Devadas, C.F. Andrews and press correspondents
at Marseilles, France in 1931

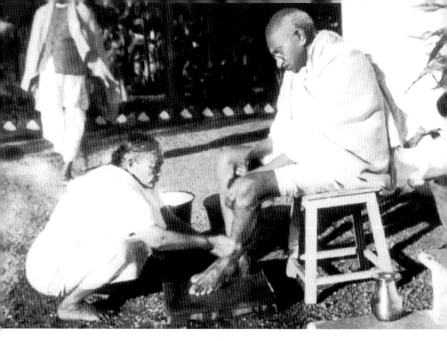

Bapu and Kasturba

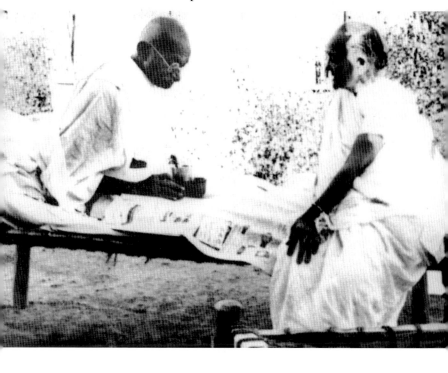

Mahatma Gandhi with Charlie Chaplin in
Canning Town, London, 1931

From left to right: Bapu, Kasturba and Badshah Gaffar Khan

Mahatma Gandhi with Mira Bhen, Devadas Gandhi, and
English friends in London, 1931

Mahatma Gandhi with Rabindranath Tagore

Mahatma Gandhi with Jawaharlal Nehru and
Maulana Azad in Wardha, 1935

Mahatma Gandhi with Netaji Subhash
Chandra Bose, 1938

Mahatma Gandhi, Kasturba and Rabindranath Tagore
at Shantiniketan,1940

Mahatma Gandhi with Sardar Patel and Maulana Abdul Kalam
Azad at the AICC meeting, Mumbai, 1940

Mahatma Gandhi with Mira Bhen, Sewagram, 1941

Aga Khan Palace in Pune where Bapu, Kasturba and Mahadev Desai had
been under house arrest from 1942-44, and this is where Kasturba died in 1944

Jinnah receiving Mahatma Gandhi in Bombay,1944

Mahatma Gandhi with Pandit Nehru at the AICC
meeting in Bombay, 1946

Telecom Italia Advertisement Poster from 2004 saying 'Imagine the world today if he could have communicated like this.'
Reprinted by kind permission of Telecom Italia.

SE AVESSE POTUTO COMUNICARE COSÌ, OGGI CHE MONDO SAREBBE?

memories of mother organizing the Shimla trip. She ensured the packing of essential utensils for use in the kitchen in Shimla. This included a rolling pin, a pair of tongs, knife, etc. A brass bucket and a small brass pot (*lota*) were also among the essential items. Pillows, bedsheets, quilts and blankets were stuffed into three or four holdalls. And then, mother must have packed a month's supplies for Gopu as well.

It was my first experience of the Himalayas. After reaching Shimla we ate – Mohan, Ramu, Sumi and I – and went to meet Bapu-ji. I distinctly remember that it was a long winding route we took, lined with Deodhar trees, monkeys playing on the branches. Sometimes we would laugh and sometimes be scared of them. At other times, we would display great courage and pass by the trees. It was such a joy to meet Bapu-ji outside jails, under the open clear skies, so much so that I did not register Ba's absence.

Ba's death was a personal loss to me. I felt this loss was mine alone. At that young age, with a natural selfishness, I was insensitive to everyone's loss, be it my parents', siblings' or anyone else's. I was just a careless eleven-year-old.

I was incapable of understanding Bapu-ji's mental or spiritual challenges, but yes, the practical approach towards familial or social issues that my grandfather showed, somehow made up for my grandmother's absence. Bapu-ji and his companions were staying at Rajkumari Amrit Kaur's house. The weather was totally unreliable even for a walk from our house to Bapu-ji's place. One minute it would be clear skies with a bright sun and the next it would start pouring. Without a care in the world, we would walk away many a time with no umbrella nor raincoats. We used to reach Bapu-ji completely drenched. This would be a cause of great worry to Bapu-ji. But without Bapu-ji saying a word, Rajkumari Amrit Kaur would arrange for us to get out of our wet clothes and have them dried. We would be made to sit in front of heaters then, wrapped in big sheets while our clothes would be drying. Often, clothes of appropriate sizes would be found for us in the house. I remember once wearing a long shirt and waiting for my clothes to dry. When my frock had dried, I wore it back again and went to Bapu-ji's room where I found him looking at the watch while many leaders were waiting in the other room to accompany Bapu-ji to the prayer meeting.

'My frock is dry now, so even I shall go with you to the prayer meeting,' I told Bapu-ji.

'Tara, we should be careful about one thing. You children should keep a set of clothes and towel here. It can rain anytime. It's not right that the Rajkumari be inconvenienced when you come. We are her guests.'

I don't remember his exact words, but I have tried to convey what Bapu-ji meant. His gentle yet firm words taught me the responsibility that being a guest entailed. This was yet another lesson in social etiquette that Bapu-ji taught me.

That period of India's freedom struggle is for me intangibly linked to Bapu-ji's teachings. In the last six decades of my life, at home or away, I have come to deeply understand the true meaning of my grandfather's words, and remember them fondly.

Those vacations in Shimla were altogether a new experience. In the sylvan surroundings of the Himalayas, the first rays of independence seemed to be closer than ever before. We saw a new side to our grandfather. Also, being eleven meant a big deal to me. For the first time, I became aware of my maternal instinct in the form of my love for my baby brother, Gopu.

My maternal uncle had brought with him an English translation of Victor Hugo's *Les Misérables*. He would read it every day and then tell us the story. This was my first introduction to Western literature and civilization.

A Muslim family lived in one of the neighbouring houses. We were very friendly with the children. They reminded us of the Pandyas, our neighbours in Delhi. We were overjoyed with our new friends, and it is here that we got our first lessons in Urdu language and Muslim culture. There was an old aunt in that family who constantly smoked the hookah. I told my friend that I also wanted to try the hookah and with her help I did so a few times. This escapade remained a secret between my friend and me. Back then, I was assailed by pangs of guilt, but today I can laugh off that childish escapade. Unfortunately, I have forgotten my friend's name. I had no intentions of confessing my misdeed to my parents or to Bapu-ji. Had I mentioned it to Bapu-ji, the memory of it would have been very different.

We would often have the privilege of walking with Bapu-ji among Shimla's crowds, and would sit with him in his community prayer meetings. I did not know the *shlokas* from the Gita nor did I understand the Koran or the Buddhist prayers. But all those chantings left an indelible mark on me. 'I will definitely learn these chants as well as the correct way to say them' – this would be my constant resolve. My siblings and I would join in the hymns and the *Ramdhun*. This signalled the awakening of spirituality in me.

Valmiki Ashram

❧

What is known as Mandir Marg today used to be earlier called Redding Road. I was studying in the Standard VII of St. Thomas School situated on Redding Road. This is in the 1940s. Miss Jerwood, the principal, a soft-hearted, delicate-looking English missionary was greatly opposed to the freedom movement.

One day, she announced, 'Mahatma Gandhi is coming to Delhi and is going to stay in a *basti* (Harijan settlement) near the school.' The school came alive with this unbelievable and thrilling piece of news. The whole day, my schoolmates kept coming intermittently to give me this news. I couldn't believe my ears and kept asking, 'Are you sure? Tell me honestly, is Bapu-ji really going to stay in the ghetto next to the school?' It was true, but I was eager to go home and confirm the news with my parents. As luck would have it, school got over early that day. This news infused new vigour and enthusiasm into a school that was trying hard to ignore and remain unaffected by the freedom movement and Gandhian thought.

The country was not yet free, but the school seemed

to have become liberated. I have mentioned the principal being opposed to the freedom movement and the school being untouched by Gandhian thought. But it would be unfair not to mention the virtues that Miss Jerwood and the school taught me.

I learnt to incorporate the moral, social and human values that I imbibed at this school not only at an intellectual level but also in my everyday life. These principles were essentially no different from the Gandhian thought. Miss Jerwood was a protestant and a great patriot who was devoted to her country. For her, to even try and comprehend India's freedom movement and the Gandhian thought would have amounted to blasphemy. And, I believe, that is the reason why she kept herself away from the events around her. The school was a reflection of her personality.

In the context of India's history, I find this description of my school strange and unnatural. But the values that I learned in the anti-Gandhi school were literally an echo of Gandhi's principles. Today, sixty years after Independence, these basic values are now disappearing.

A Muslim girl used to sit next to me in class. The daughter of the British government's commander-in-chief and the daughters of the Hindu driver of a British officer were also my classmates. One of my brightest classmates was the daughter of a Kashmiri ICS officer as were the daughters of middle-class Iyer and Iyengar Tamil Brahmins. One of my closest friends was a cultured Punjabi girl. We were both very fond of playing the sitar. Staunch Hindu girls were close friends with burqa-clad Muslim girls in my school. A girl belonging to a well-known Kayastha family also studied in my class. We were bound together in our Indianness, our values and cultures, and our affinity with nature. Like girls of our age, we swore allegiance to each other forever. We did not have a school uniform; we wore frocks, salwar-kameezes, gararas and saris according to our customs and fancy. But there was a definite dignity to our actions and values.

Our school was part of the St. Thomas Church on Redding Road. I don't recall ever being forced to worship in the church. I did not ever hear any talk of conversion to Christianity. Even though we hailed from varied cultural milieus, we were accepted unconditionally.

I found the beautiful school church fascinating. There was an aura of mystery about it. The silence inside intrigued me a lot; it seemed to have an extraordinary power. Miss Jerwood never compelled us to go to the church, lest it be misconstrued by the students' families. A couple of times, a few of us took permission from her and went to the church during recess. The interior of the church was always redolent of the scent of wood and melting candles. The candles seemed to dispel all mystery. There was a sense of familiarity in the church as it was a symbol of the same devotion and belief that exist within all of us. It stood for the faith that keeps us anchored to our roots and, in all our diversity, gives us identity.

My first experience of attending a church wedding was when all the students were invited to one of our Christian teacher's wedding in this very church. I saw a strict teacher in a new light, as a charming and beautiful bride. The customary Christian gown, long and white, was exquisite.

Later in life, I was invited to many church weddings, here and abroad. However, the memory of that wedding in St. Thomas Church will always remain special. I had never seen a church wedding before. As the couple came out of the church and all of us gathered around them to offer our felicitations, I turned around instinctively and looked inside the church. The glow of a candle flame seemed to be sending me a spiritual message.

I have another recollection of the church. One of our classmates was absent for a few days. When she rejoined school, she told us that her mother had passed away after a long illness. She said that before her death, her mother had called all her children, prayed with them and blessed them. 'Mother had tears of farewell in her eyes,' she said and burst out crying. Looking at her, we couldn't stop ourselves from crying either. It seemed to be a part of destiny's plan that a young girl find solace in recounting the heartrending account of her mother's demise. A prayer meeting was held for her mother in our school church. In her poignant account, in the church service as well as in the cycle of life and death, maternal love was the all-prevalent emotion.

In that moment of revelation, the school church's aura of mystery was dispelled. There was no mystery anymore – only truth and compassion. At that young age, I was incapable of intellectually analysing my emotions. Today, I truly understand the depth of that experience.

I was overjoyed the day I heard that Mahatma Gandhi was coming to Delhi, and would be staying in the *basti* near the school. It was unbelievable, but the news was true.

Bapu-ji arrived a couple of days later. As planned, he stayed in the *basti*. There was an air of festivity in the school. As soon as I came to know that Bapu-ji had arrived, I became restless with excitement to go visit my grandfather. In all my haste, I did not go home after school; it was as if I had grown wings and I flew to meet Bapu-ji. There were many volunteers posted outside the *basti*, but in those days, security arrangements were nowhere close to what it is today.

I am not sure whether my neighbours, the Pandya sisters, were with me. There's only a vague recollection of some friends being with me. I greeted Bapu-ji, and with great excitement said, 'Bapu-ji, I study in the school right next door. I am coming directly from there.' Bapu-ji smiled. He knew about my school. Appa (Father) must have met him earlier and informed him.

I was aware of the bond between the father and the son. I had witnessed this closeness in my teenage years when Bapu-ji once stayed with us for some time. I came to understand the support an adoring son offered his father. In Appa's selfless devotion to his father, there was a certain purity and a strong sense of responsibility.

Bapu-ji said, 'I have heard that your school has a playground. Can I go there for a walk in the evenings? Ask your principal. If she allows, I could walk there after my evening prayers.'

I ran back to the school. My principal was still there. I told her about Bapu-ji's request. Softly she said, 'Yes, yes. Your grandfather can use our playground for his walk.' Her permission made me realize that she had not allowed her personal feelings to cloud her judgment. Of course, that may just have been my imagination. I went straight to Bapu-ji to give him the good news. I felt proud to have succeeded in a task entrusted to me by him.

I don't know what we studied in school during those weeks. The whole day would be spent in anticipation of meeting Bapu-ji. Sometimes we met him more than once in a day. I would meet him after school, and then again, in the evening, mother would take us all along with the Pandya sisters for the evening prayers. On Sundays, we would go there in the morning. And, I would go there at eight thirty or nine in the night as well with my father. It was a time that was both convenient and important for my father and Bapu-ji. By eight p.m., a cot would be laid out for Bapu-ji in the veranda outside, under the clear night sky. Bapu-ji needed only a white *khadi* sheet, a pillow and a mosquito net for his sleep. Never before had there been a bed as pure and pristine as this one with its coarse *khadi* sheet. I would sit at the edge of the bed and press my grandfather's feet.

Though I accompanied my father on his insistence, the father and son would be so engrossed in their discussions that they would forget about my being there. It was as if I were invisible. They would converse in Gujarati and, as far as I can remember, the topic of conversation would always be family issues, away from the realm of politics and philosophy. Some of my father's questions were always the same: 'Bapu, you should be careful with your diet. What did you eat today? How much did you manage to rest in the day today? How is your digestion these days? How many people came to meet you? Who all? How long was your discourse after the prayers?' Bapu-ji was always surrounded by his companions and my father was a part of their joys, sorrows and problems. In Bapu-ji's soft voice, simple language and his humour, I sensed him letting go of all his troubles.

Although I was young, I was aware that it was a privilege for me to be there. But I did not know that those moments would forever be imprinted on my precious memory, and that even in my old age, I would turn to them for guidance.

Were Bapu-ji and Appa aware that those moments would become a priceless treasure for me?

Bapu-ji would sleep only after I pressed his feet. Today, when I think about it, I wonder what was the significance of pressing Mahatma Gandhi's aching feet and have him surrender to my ministrations and fall asleep. Maybe this was Bapu-ji's way of acknowledging his familial bonds. Two minutes of talking to his son, a bit of advice, a bit of fun, and getting his granddaughter to press his feet – these were moments of familial intimacy for Bapu-ji.

The experience of being in close contact with Bapu-ji in Shimla, then meeting him regularly near my school and later, after Independence, spending the last four months of his life with him in Birla House on Albuquerque Road were a blessing for me from that extraordinary era.

During the time I spent with him at the *basti*, Bapu-ji saw through my immaturity and his efforts to educate me increased. He did not talk of philosophy, meditation or the freedom struggle. He would talk of behaviour, etiquettes, games, entertainment, language learning, handwriting and creative education for children. There would be no fixed time or place for Bapu-ji's sermons. Sometimes, he would instruct with a smile, sometimes in jest, and at other times, he would be dead serious. Often, it felt like a reprimand, but it always seemed right, and I always understood. I realized the strength of his personality during this period.

Once, we were to go to my paternal grandparents' house. From Madras we were to go to Kuttralam to see the waterfalls there. That day, before the evening prayers, Bapu-ji said to me laughingly, 'I have heard that all of you are going to have some fun for a few days. You will meet Anna (we called our maternal grandfather Anna). Learn

Tamil well and then teach me. Enjoy yourself bathing under the waterfalls.'

For a few moments, I was left staring at my grandfather. I could not believe his enthusiasm. This way he became a part of our holiday. 'Write to me,' he said. I don't remember if I wrote to him. But once earlier, I had written a letter to him and his comments on my bad handwriting had totally crushed me. Bapu-ji had written to me, 'I received your letter. It's not nice. Improve your handwriting and write to me again.' Angry and hurt, I tore the letter to pieces. I did not realize then how precious a historical document a postcard in Bapu-ji's writing would ever be. I don't think I ever wrote to Bapu-ji again after that. I lost out on some interesting discourse as a result. There was no exchange of letters with Bapu-ji, but I did spend more time with him.

There was a certain element of fun in being educated by Bapu-ji. But sometimes we would be inattentive too. Once, after the prayer meeting, Bapu-ji said to me, 'You should single-mindedly think of God during prayers.'

I probably deserved the rebuke. But I still explained to him, 'Bapu-ji, I pray with a lot of concentration.'

'Okay, then tell me what were the words to the hymn sung today?'

He seemed to be challenging me – and I was caught out. My mind was constantly engaged in different things. I could recall the rhythm of the hymn but not the words.

He only said, 'While praying you should pay attention to the words of the prayer' and nothing further. After this incident, I resolved to learn all the prayers and hymns. But Bapu-ji never brought up the subject again, and so my strife remained mine alone.

It was at that time at the Valmiki Ashram that I took

my one-and-a-half-year-old brother Gopu to meet Bapu-ji. When little Gopu said 'Dada, Dada', Bapu-ji was overcome with emotion. 'All of you call me Bapu-ji, but you must teach Gopu to say Dada.'

Gopu was adorable. Bapu-ji would joke with him and say, 'Gopu, what does Dada say?' Gopu would put a finger on his lips and lisp, 'Teep tuiet, don't phite and teep peace.' That smile, that laughter was meant to be shared only between a grandfather and his grandson. My mother later remembered the times when Bapu-ji would forget everything and everyone in his joy of seeing Gopu. She was right. The moments he spent with Gopu would relieve him of all his tensions.

Once, there was a conversation about the kitchen. 'Do you know how to boil water?' Bapu-ji suddenly asked me. 'Yes, Bapu-ji. Why wouldn't a girl my age know how to boil water?' I should have said that I did not know any household chores but, sitting on high moral ground, my effort to impress my grandfather was a reflection of my immaturity. 'You have to get the fire ready before boiling water. You should know how to light a wood and coal stove.' In those days, there were no gas stoves in Delhi. Bapu-ji always talked of getting the basics right. He knew that his son's young, spoilt daughter would not know the basics. I was useless in a kitchen before I set up my own household.

Years later, when my husband lovingly taught me how to light a stove and boil rice, I thought of my grandfather: *'To boil water one must know how to light a stove.'*

Every action that Gandhi portrayed was a reflection of his beliefs. And that is why every wish that he expressed – however small – was a command for us, a religion to be followed.

Whatever he told us would be accompanied by his trademark laughter. One day Bapu-ji said to me, 'Your father is an editor in a newspaper and you must be getting a lot of letters at home. Don't throw away those envelopes. Open them and make a sheaf of the clean sides for me to write on.' My brothers and I were highly motivated and began to collect the envelopes for him. We split them open, put the clean sides up, made a pile and showed it to Appa. My father trimmed those envelopes and said, 'Bapu-ji likes everything to be done neatly.' There was a lesson in this – a lesson to use time wisely and to recycle waste products, to complete a task properly and learning the joys of working in a group. In the entire episode, I saw my father's understanding of and adoration for his own father. When we took that neat little pile to Bapu-ji, he was thrilled. His smile was reward enough for us. Taking the neatly trimmed envelopes, he smiled and said, 'I can see your father's contribution in this.' Why wouldn't a father recognize the result of his teachings to his son?

To achieve one's goals, it's essential to think of children as an important part of one's life and to keep them motivated. In the search for truth, a young mind is a great leveller. Bapu-ji was always enthusiastic about making us children an integral part of nation building, and that thought is the foundation of our national spirit even today.

Bapu-ji had a lot of warmth for his family. At the same time, I felt that he gave my friends as much importance as he did to his grandchildren. On the other hand, because we were so close to the Pandya sisters it seemed natural and acceptable for them to be equally close to Bapu-ji. None of Bapu-ji's four sons or daughters-in-law is alive today. Amongst the grandchildren, we are now five brothers and four sisters.[1] All of us have our own memories of our grandfather.

Bapu-ji was close to people outside the family as well. He had an uncanny ability to understand them. He would be serious as well as jocular depending on a person's strengths and weaknesses.

At Valmiki Ashram, we had the opportunity of meeting and getting to know the most influential and extraordinary people linked to the freedom movement. But I did not realize the importance of those people then.

Being a devoted disciple gave Pandit Nehru the liberty of visiting Bapu-ji anytime. It was a rare and wonderful relationship between them – of a teacher and disciple. It was made up of Nehru's adoration and Mahatma Gandhi's affection. I remember Pandit Nehru as being a bit preoccupied at Valmiki Ashram. The country was not yet free and talk of Partition was spreading fast. But everybody involved in the freedom struggle was invigorated by how close Independence was.

My siblings and I and a few other people had free access to Bapu-ji. Praveena Pandya also felt very free to speak with Bapu-ji. She was the eldest and the most mature amongst us, and would surprise us with the temerity with which she asked questions.

Once, while walking in the playground at St. Thomas School, Praveena asked Bapu-ji, 'Does Pandit-ji love children as much as you do?' Bapu-ji did not pull her ears. He answered gravely, 'You don't know him and that's why you are asking me that. If you get a chance to get to know him, you will realize that he loves children more than I

[1] This piece was written before the sudden death of the writer's younger brother Prof. Ramchandra Gandhi in June 2007.

do.' At that very moment, Badshah Khan was approaching us. 'Do you know who that is, coming this way?' Bapu-ji asked.

'Badshah Khan is so tall. How do we talk to him? We would need a ladder to talk to him,' replied Praveena.

'You are very naughty,' Bapu-ji laughed and pulled her ear.

We had known Frontier Gandhi (Badshah Khan) for a long time. I have very fond memories from when I was very small of Maulana Azad, Sardar Patel, my maternal grandfather Shri Rajagopalachari, and Badshah Khan.

A group of Pathans would come to our house with Badshah Khan. They were seated around the table and served food. There would be a lot of seasonal fruit. 'We don't know what kind of food they eat so we should provide plenty of fruit, milk and curds for them,' Mother would say. I guess what mother meant was that they were probably used to a non-vegetarian diet and would be inconvenienced by the vegetarian food we served.[2]

I was just a bit taller than the table then. I would stand next to Badshah Khan and ask my mother, 'Why does he drink milk from such a big pot?' Badshah Khan would smile and explain to me, 'All Pathans drink milk from big pots.' Father would smile but my mother would rebuke me gently. It was bad manners to comment on how much and what the guests chose to eat. I distinctly remember that when Badshah Khan was a guest in our house, Mother would herself wash his clothes. Such were the rules and responsibilities of hospitality to a guest in those days.

I went to meet Badshah Khan in a Delhi hospital in

---

[2] The writer does not know for sure if Badshah Khan was a vegetarian or a non-vegetarian.

1987 when he was ill. He was still as attractive and his personality as fascinating as ever. But I could not tell him the tale of the milk, the pot and the Pathans. It was sometime after Badshah Khan's death in 1988 that I went to Pakistan. My daughter Sukanya also accompanied me. I met Badshah Khan's family in Peshawar and they looked after us wonderfully, in true Pakistani style. When they came to know of my interest in hand-woven *khadi*, they pulled out and gave me yards of khaddar as a present; there was a strong smell of earthiness in every thread of that coarse cloth. It was a priceless gift.

Today when I think of Valmiki Ashram in Delhi, I am overwhelmed with memories of Badshah Khan with Bapu-ji and they evoke these words: *Pathan, Pakistan, friendship, smell of khadi, and a pot of milk.*

Valmiki Ashram was witness to unprecedented historical moments on the eve of Independence in 1946-47.

Gandhi's mighty revolution was dynamic in nature. It was a spontaneous movement. The common man stood helpless in the wake of the torrents of revolution sweeping through the country. Gandhi was motivating everybody to experiment with their truths. I am not saying this with the authority of a historian or that of a psychologist. My thoughts and observations are based on the past that today resonates within me.

A young twelve-year-old girl became aware of an epoch-making history unfolding in Delhi's Valmiki Ashram. The girl could obviously not foresee then how she would analyse or understand those feelings later in life. My experiences at twelve years of age and my deep understanding of those very experiences in my seventh decade are two halves of my reality.

Meeting influential people from that extraordinary era was taken for granted by us as children. People from all walks of life would come to Bapu-ji. Everyone had a question in their eyes: *How, when will we get freedom*? These questions agitated everybody's mind. This restlessness was but natural in the last unsure moments of the freedom movement.

Bapu-ji's room in Valmiki Ashram was medium sized. The atmosphere was what we were used to. Wherever Bapu-ji may have stayed, an ashram, a jail or a train compartment, there was always a sanctity about that place; a purity of light, sound and smell. Gandhi's spiritual devotion and humane spirit would keep his surroundings pristine and alive.

The simplicity of Gandhi's actions, thought and food was a reflection of his ideals. His purity was so overpowering that I would hesitate to pick up even his slippers. His slippers would be cleaner than my hands and I would be scared of dirtying them. Bapu-ji would touch even inanimate objects so gently it seemed as if they too had souls. Every time I dispose of trash, I think of my grandfather and the dignity with which he would do the task.

I think there was one electric fan in Bapu-ji's room in the ashram. The thin mattress on the floor was covered with a white *khadi* sheet, and next to it would always be a spinning wheel. There would always be a pillow against the wall, and Bapu-ji would sit up straight supported by it. His *khadi* did not have the shiny whiteness of the *khadi* of today; it was a natural whiteness born of hard manual labour. A low table on the floor was used by Bapu-ji to read and write on. Bapu-ji was connected to the world through letters, postcards, messages and opinions.

Today when I think about it, I wonder how a table belonging to such a busy man could have been so tidy all the time. There was never any pile on that table. I have a shiny table in my office – the mark of a successful and busy officer; there are cupboards full of books; there is a sofa and a television; my secretary's room has computers and all the modern equipment possible. Yet, my svelte glass-top table is unable to solve my problems or resolve issues. Mahatma Gandhi will always be the guiding light of our lives.

I don't remember him ever being anxious during his stay at Valmiki Ashram, even though the times were very tense. His other half, his life partner Kasturba's passing had given him unbearable pain. It had left him bereaved, yet he did not retire nor give up. He continued searching for truth relentlessly. The spiritual meaning of his diligence came across in his humane smile; at least that is how I understand it today.

Bapu-ji and his companions would have learned discussions about Satyagrah, but I was intellectually incapable of absorbing them then. My age was not to be blamed for this. I have always been more intuitive than intellectual. Intuition is what made me aware of the importance of the freedom movement. Even in the serious deliberations of Satyagrah, Bapu-ji's virtues of truth, compassion and humour made him seem maternal. Bapu-ji's maternal attitude towards me in Valmiki Ashram probably came from a sense of responsibility towards Kasturba. As a result of these experiences, I now believe that maternal power is unparalleled in Gandhian philosophy and the spinning wheel is also a part of this very philosophy. This is a conclusion based on a life that has been devoted to understanding the Gandhian philosophy.

Life with Bapu-ji in Valmiki Ashram also revealed a few bitter truths about myself. The community prayers at five in the evening were a major attraction. The prayer ground was inside the ashram. Next to the ashram was a big enclosure. There would be a huge crowd outside Bapu-ji's room. I would feel privileged to walk with Bapu-ji to the ground. While walking, Bapu-ji would take the support of a girl. All the children there and the adults as well wanted to be the one to give him support as he walked. All of us would compete with each other to be Bapu-ji's girl. I had got used to being the chosen one, but sometimes other girls would beat me to it. One evening when I walked out with Bapu-ji, I saw Vijay Lakshmi Pandit waiting to meet Bapu-ji with her two good-looking daughters. They greeted Bapu-ji and I don't know why I moved aside. At that point, Bapu-ji said to me, 'They are our special guests so let them be my girls today, and you stay with me on the way back from the prayers.' Both the sisters were cultured and very virtuous. Bapu-ji introduced them to me. They put Bapu-ji's hands on their shoulders very gracefully, and looked at me with apologetic eyes. On many occasions, Bapu-ji would give preference to outsiders. It used to upset me a lot, and I would always resent and wonder why he loved others in the same way that he cared for us, his own grandchildren. Admitting this openly to others would have made me seem very small, so I never did that. Today I understand that this was Bapu-ji's strength and what made him the 'Father of the Nation'.

There is a very amusing anecdote that I would like to share. Once, when we came out of Bapu-ji's room to go for the prayer meeting, I saw a guest from Britain separate himself from the crowd and approach Bapu-ji. Bapu-ji had probably been waiting for him. He stopped to greet the British guest. It was Sir Stafford Cripps. He had come to India on a special mission related to India's independence, but I was completely oblivious to the historical context of this special visit.

Talking about those contexts and issues today would mean venturing into unfamiliar territory. But I cannot forget this rather amusing episode. Bapu-ji introduced me to Sir Stafford Cripps with the pride of a grandfather. 'Please meet my granddaughter, my youngest son's daughter.'

'How do you do?' Saying so, Sir Stafford Cripps put out his hand.

In the twelve years of my life I had never shaken hands with an Englishman. Though English was spoken in school and at home and I did speak it a bit, in the excitement of shaking hands with an Englishman I not only thought it necessary to answer him but also thought it to be my prerogative to do so.

'Oh I had fever yesterday. I am feeling better today. Tomorrow I will go to school, but I am not sure. If there is no ache in my body, my mother will allow me to go to school.' It was too long an answer for the greeting 'How do you do?' I took it in the sense of 'How are you?'

It was time for prayers and Bapu-ji was looking at his watch. His responsibility to the nation was above everything else. Even that historical moment was slave to his rigorous daily routine. But his young granddaughter's foolishness became unbearable for him and, momentarily forgetting his esteemed guest, he explained to me, 'Tara, when someone asks you, "How do you do?" you only say, "How do you do?" in reply. You should not talk of your health then.'

I felt hurt and rather embarrassed. When I got home, I told Mother, 'What kind of a language is this? When someone asks you how you are, shouldn't we talk about ourselves?' Bapu-ji's reprimand had rankled so much because in his code of conduct, concern for others' health was of utmost importance. This new revelation about English customs seemed totally contrary to our culture. But today, that memory is a mere source of amusement. And at times, I wonder if I did not momentarily shatter the seriousness of that historical moment.

All the children would sit near Bapu-ji's feet with an unfathomable expectation. Welcoming and meeting famous guests was a regular routine, but it never failed to arouse our curiosity. Sometimes, depending on Bapu-ji's requirements, we would have to leave the room. We didn't mind that at all; in fact we found it more fascinating. But I don't remember ever being asked to leave the room whenever Pandit Nehru came visiting. I vaguely recall seeing the then Governor General Lord Mountbatten and Lady Mountbatten with Bapu-ji.

Quaid-e-Aazam Mohammad Ali Jinnah's visit left a lasting impression on me. According to a famous historian, Jinnah never went to Valmiki Ashram. But I remember his visit clearly. The venue may be a debatable issue, but the resonance of that meeting that touched my impressionable mind cannot be denied.

Jinnah was to come and there was a lot of activity around Bapu-ji. Jinnah came. Even at that young age I could sense the inflexibility of his stance. He was polite and dressed very well. Both men were of slender build, one in a farmer's dhoti and the other, a gentleman in elegant Western attire. I felt that in his heart the Quaid-e-Aazam accepted Mahatma Gandhi's pleasing personality and his truth, but his allegiance lay elsewhere. He searched for justification and acceptance in Gandhi's affection. I have to reiterate here that this is not an opinion of a historian. These are memories of a seventy-four-year-old woman reminiscing about the time she was around twelve years of age.

My days at Valmiki Ashram are the foundation of my life. Writing about my experiences from back then has helped me to look inwards and lend clarity to my thoughts.

Birla House, 1947–48

A few days after 15 August 1947, Delhi was burning.
Before long, the flames of violence had engulfed the
city in such a way that the very foundation of one's belief
in humanity was shaken.

Schools were closed down. Our house and the newspaper
office downstairs were the hub of nervous activity. Either
there was mass hysteria or a suffocating silence on the
roads. The deathly silence would be broken intermittently
by piercing screams.

We were born and brought up in uncertain times of
struggle and strife. That is why it was natural for us to be
stoical about the circumstances. It was disturbing for me to
know that some Muslim girls from my school had left their
homes and gone elsewhere with their families. A Muslim
friend of mine used to live near the Hanuman temple.
Another one lived near the Jama Masjid. I tried hard to
meet them but in vain. We were not used to such violence.
We had been trained to fight and protest against foreign
forces. Coming face to face with our inherent violence was

a harsh reality. In those scary times, Father had to stay out late as the safety of the Muslim workers in his office was his responsibility.

The tireless whirring of the printing machine in our building was a constant reminder of the freedom struggle that was not yet over. We had won our fight against the foreign enemies, but were now faced with a long struggle against our innate aggression and social injustice. There was a familiar comfort and a promise in the continuous whirring of the machines. When the machines fell silent after work, we would suddenly wake up with trepidation. In those painful times, various businesses closed down along with schools and colleges in Delhi. It was as if stores selling food products had disappeared into thin air.

Mother would normally have a month's rations at home. We had many people staying with us, about fifty in all, counting relatives and co-workers. The situation was very serious. Today I understand how Mother must have tried in vain to shield us from the uncertainties. I was petrified all the time. 'Ma, do we have rice for dinner tonight?' I would ask. 'Don't worry. We have everything.' I would sense the anxiousness in Mother's voice. But then in the evening, when she would ask me to help her serve food, I would be reassured.

Once, she had to manage without vegetables, potatoes or onions. I could understand her anxiety. One afternoon, someone brought two baskets of potatoes out of the blue. I jumped for joy and ran to give Mother the good news. She couldn't believe it. The potatoes that day were a godsend in those difficult times of food scarcity when uncertainty prevailed over every meal. Rice and potato gravy had never tasted as good as it did that day.

We would also hear rumours, designed to ignite the already burning reality. One day some people came running and told us that a mob was advancing towards the *Hindustan Times* office. They were sure to attack our house as well. For a while, all of us were shell-shocked. Father was out and Mother either did not understand the seriousness of the situation or did not wish to alarm us. Though Mother did not seem perturbed, as a precaution I told my brothers to quickly hide under a bed. The news was a blatant rumour. Father came home and said that the situation had improved in Delhi. Things had not normalized, but there seemed to be some relief, though the embers still smouldered under the ashes.

The violence and bloodshed in the capital after Independence forced Mahatma Gandhi to leave Calcutta for Delhi. This was a blow to Delhi's self-reliance. But Gandhi's presence was the only source of solace for troubled minds. Also, at last, the sound of the printing press seemed to be carrying good news.

The day Bapu-ji came to Delhi, we ran to meet him. Mother did not go with us. Bapu-ji asked me, 'Where is Lakshmi?' When we got back, I told Mother that Bapu-ji was asking about her. 'I am very embarrassed that there has been such carnage in Delhi. How do I face Bapu-ji? How do I defend Delhi?' said Mother.

The next day, gathering all her courage, Mother went to meet Bapu-ji. She greeted him with folded hands and her head covered with her sari. Her eyes glistened with unshed tears; tears of remorse for the violence and hatred that had been unleashed in the city. The scene could have been an inspiration for a poem or a painting. I was witness to Gandhi's despair and Mother's grief.

Mother had a unique relationship with her father-in-law. She had of her own free will returned all the jewellery, clothes and other gifts she had received at her wedding. This she did in deference to Gandhi-ji's wishes. Bapu-ji had given his blessings for only one gift – an ordinary wooden box for keeping a small spindle that Mother treasured. Every time I saw that little box I would tell Mother that I wanted it. I had no interest in spinning or in that spindle; all I wanted was the box. Mother would reassure me that she had kept that box for me. Did she know that I would find my life's meaning in the spinning wheel?

I got another chance to spend time with Bapu-ji after his stay at Valmiki Ashram near my school. Irrespective of the situation, he always found time to entertain us kids. My friends at school had complained that now that the country was free, why wasn't Gandhi-ji staying at the ashram near the school? I had been told at home that it was better for him to stay at Birla House on Albuquerque Road for security reasons as the situation was still volatile.

After Independence, the atmosphere in St. Thomas had changed. Our teachers' perspectives had also changed. Miss Jerwood had gone back to England, but her values and principles still formed the foundation on which the school rested. Everyone felt the absence of her firm yet gentle and calm personality. Even on the day Miss Jerwood was leaving, she had bent to pick up a scrap of paper from the ground and had told us with equanimity, 'Whenever you see garbage, always pick it up. Garbage should be thrown in dustbins.' Her language may have been English, but it reflected the universal values of life and society. Even today, St. Thomas Church and the school on Mandir Marg are exactly as I remember them.

During the evening walks with Bapu-ji at Birla House, I was reminded of my school playground at St. Thomas. I once commented that the school playground was more appropriate for an evening walk. He gently chided me that one should always exercise and walk unmindful of the place being big or small. The big garden in Birla House was kept ready for the evening community prayers. Next to the garden was a covered strip of land, suitable for Bapu-ji's walk. Even in rain we would walk for at least half an hour.

It was during that time that I overheard Mother say, 'Bapu-ji seems to have become orphaned after Ba's death. Manu and Abha leave no stone unturned in looking after him. We also make every effort to look after him but... His clothes aren't as clean as they used to be. Even his diet is not as regulated and he doesn't rest enough.' These words uttered unconsciously by Ma left a strong impression on me. But I couldn't understand where she was falling short in serving Bapu-ji and why she had sounded so full of remorse. There was a hint of helplessness in her voice.

Bapu-ji's stay at Valmiki Ashram too had come after Ba's passing, but he had been excited and motivated then. He was the navigator then, steering his country ashore through stormy seas. In Birla House he had to admit that he had reached the shore, but the path to his final destination was still long and rough. Gandhi was dejected by the naked truth of man's depraved mind and the sadness of the country's division. My fourteen-year-old mind was pained by my grandfather's anguish.

Bapu-ji continued to treat me the same way that he had in Valmiki Ashram. Back then I felt that I was entitled to his affection, but today I realize that it was borne out of a sense of duty. Dinner was between seven and seven thirty p.m.

at Birla House. My brothers and I would always be there. Manu Behen and Abha Bhabhi would take Gopu with them to feed him. We would also be asked to join for dinner. We loved the excellent vegetarian food that was served. Bapu-ji explained to me that in the Birla family tradition, guests were very well looked after. But it was our responsibility to ensure that we did not take undue advantage of that; only little Gopu should eat there. It was acceptable for Manu Bhen, Abha Bhabhi and a few others who lived with Bapu-ji to eat there, but we ought to have eaten at home. He was right and we did just that though I did disobey Bapu-ji's wishes a couple of times. I would go with Gopu to the first floor to meet Ghanshyam Das Birla's daughter-in-law, Sarla Behen. She was extremely fond of us. 'I am arranging for food for Gopu and you right here. You eat here and then go home,' she would say. I never declined her affectionate invitation. Bapu-ji understood everything but never said a word to me. However, this whole experience taught me the responsibilities that being a host and a guest entailed.

At that young age, I was interested in dressing up, though not in the most tasteful way. I always wore *khadi*, but my earrings would be garish and elaborate. 'Why do you need to wear these? You will be a lot freer without these and look more beautiful,' Bapu-ji would pull my ears and say, half in jest and half seriously. In his observation lay a command, but I did not pay any heed, not even for the sake of pretence. I could not free myself of that frivolity. Today, I have overcome such desires, though I loved colours then and love them even now. Even my *khadi* clothes those days would have a splash of colour, but Bapu-ji never commented on my taste.

Recently, a reporter remarked, 'Being Bapu-ji's grand-daughter, shouldn't you be wearing white *khadi*? Why are you so fond of colours?'

'The colours of the Earth are an integral part of me. How do I explain that in the whiteness of Gandhi's *khadi* I see all these colours,' I said. Laughingly I added, 'It would be unfair to use Gandhi's standards as a yardstick to judge me for I will always lose. You need to look at me as an ordinary individual.'

People from all walks of life would find it natural to voice their dissenting opinions frankly in front of Bapu-ji. Those who were inspired by *khadi* chose to wear it. But Bapu-ji accepted even those who were unaccustomed to *khadi* and wore other fabric. I never saw Bapu-ji lose his temper nor talk condescendingly to anyone. A person would always feel respected in Bapu-ji's presence. Bapu-ji's advice would always fall within the realm of the mental and physical capabilities of the person.

In those days, we were very friendly with a well-known ICS officer's daughter. She thought of us as family and was very inspired by Gandhian thought. Though she always wore georgette or chiffon saris and went to the club regularly, she would go with us every day to meet Bapu-ji. She would remove her stylish sandals outside Bapu-ji's room and go quietly sit in a corner. I kept waiting for Bapu-ji to ask her why she did not wear *khadi*. I was curious to hear her response, but Bapu-ji never commented on her clothes.

This curiosity was satisfied a few years after Bapu-ji's death. The friend had got married and divorced soon after. Then we came to know that she had renounced the world and become a *sadhvi*. We were a little disconcerted by the

fact that we had never really understood her. Only Bapu-ji
had been able to look beyond her veneer of clothing and
sense her search for inner peace. It is through episodes like
this that I understand Bapu-ji better today.

We spent the first Diwali of independent India with
Bapu-ji. The day after Diwali is celebrated as the Gujarati
New Year. This day had such significance for my father that
he asked Bapu-ji to specially address the Gujarati residents
of Delhi at Birla House. I remember how he had persuaded
Bapu-ji with reason and logic that if he were to address the
Gujarati community it would mean the world to all those
people. Bapu-ji agreed with a smile.

That New Year, a large number of Gujaratis congregated
for Bapu-ji's prayer meeting. He spoke in Gujarati and
ushered in the New Year. I don't remember what he said
in his address. With convincing arguments and the liberty
only a son could take, Father had managed to get Bapu-ji
to perform this social obligation.

There is an unforgettable incident related to one of
India's finest singers, M.S. Subbulakshmi, that I need to
recount. One day when I got back from school, my father
said, 'Taru, M.S. Subbulakshmi has come to Delhi from
Madras with her family, and she wants to sing a *bhajan* for
Bapu-ji before the evening prayers. Her daughter Radha
will dance to her *bhajan*. You have to take these esteemed
guests to Bapu-ji and organize their performance after
taking his permission.' I was very excited to be performing
such an important task. I did not bother changing out of
my school uniform, nor my slippers, one of which was
broken. I went to Bapu-ji with the guests. As always he was
sitting up straight on his mattress. He was busy writing. I
went close to him and said, 'Bapu-ji, Appa has said that

M.S. Subbulakshmi wishes to sing a *bhajan* for you, and her daughter will dance along.'

There may have been a slight smile on his face. Without putting down his pen he said, 'She is most welcome to sing and her daughter can dance, but they must forgive me because I will only listen and not watch as I am writing.' M.S. Subbulakshmi started singing a hymn from her popular film, *Meera* – '*Ghanshyam ayo ri, mere ghar shyam ayo ri*' – as her young daughter Radha danced. Little Gopu also crawled in, swaying to the music. Bapu-ji put his pen down. He listened and watched, sitting still. As soon as the hymn was over, he got up and looked at his watch. He walked up to M.S. Subbulakshmi and softly requested her, 'It is now time for prayers and today you shall sing the *bhajans*.' M.S. Subbulakshmi's voice rang through the prayers that evening. There was an appreciation for a great artiste in Bapu-ji's words and in his voice.

The community prayers every evening in Birla House used to be the high point of the day. It was as if the whole day was organized around them. In a way it was a moment of spiritual refuge. After the pan-religion prayer and the singing of *Ramdhun*, Bapu-ji would give a discourse. Even for those who were not a part of the prayer meeting, his discourse served as a challenge to the directionless and complacent consciousness of mankind. His thoughts on the country, society and politics were inspired by his eternal search for truth. Gandhi's heart had been ripped by the injustice and violence that had been unleashed by people on each other. He would stress on the principles of truth and non-violence. These values of truth and non-violence were such a strong part of our lives that the moment we reached Bapu-ji, we would be soaked in the all-pervading

Gandhian philosophy and would try to live by it to the best of our abilities.

Gandhi would make meticulous changes in his diet and attire according to requirement. I always saw him eat very little and I was very influenced by his eating habits. He would eat with a spoon from a biggish bowl and I saw him eat mostly fruits, boiled vegetables and gruel.

He donned a labourer's attire in the last few decades of his life; he wore knee–length, hand-spun dhoti; to shield himself from the sun or the cold, he used a cotton shawl. I never saw Bapu-ji wearing stitched clothes; not even socks. I often wonder today how he weathered the Delhi cold without socks and with his chest bare. Was this an example of the spiritual strength of an Indian labourer?

Even this description cannot convey a complete sense of Bapu-ji's personality. Even his full-throated, lively laughter was an example of his purity. His fascinating smile would keep us children enthralled.

We had the wonderful experience of meeting well-known people from all walks of life – Pandit Jawaharlal Nehru, Sardar Patel, Maulana Azad, Dr. Rajendra Prasad, and C. Rajagopalachari. Unmindful of their stature, all these great people would sit with Bapu-ji, on the sheet spread on the floor.

I could have written a diary, but I was interested in other things. Manu Behen used to write a diary regularly. She made no claims to be an intellectual, a literary writer or a historian. She used to write it as a daily task that was part of the Gandhian way of life, and her diary went on to become the basis of many researches later. Many a time, I wanted to be like my paternal cousin, Manu.

I was also impressed by another woman. I was very

taken with Rajkumari Amrit Kaur's slim silhouette draped in a fine *khadi* sari and her elegance. I found her *khadi* so exquisite that I decided to always wear *khadi*. That ultramodern lady was inspired by Gandhi. With her head covered, she would translate Gandhi's discourse into English on the spot. I would keep admiring her beautiful hands. The way she held the Sheaffers and the Parker in her hand would make for a successful advertisement. Here, I would like to mention something strange that happened fifty years later.

I met a college friend after many years. She had become a theatre artist. 'It is so nice to meet you, Tara,' she said. 'I want to give you some *khadi* saris that I was given when I played Rajkumari Amrit Kaur.'

'Why do you want to give them to me?' I asked curiously.

'These are the saris that Rajkumari Amrit Kaur had herself worn. I got them, but I think you deserve them more than I do.' I was speechless. Saris belonging to a princess of an Indian royal family, saris that were of the finest *khadi*, and that belonged in a museum had somehow found their way to me after so many years. My heart said this happened because, as a young girl, I had really coveted those saris.

When I was with Bapu-ji at Birla House, I would want to be like Manu Behen. At other times, I wanted to be like Rajkumari Amrit Kaur. But the truth was that I was just an immature, lazy schoolgirl, and all I wanted was freedom from school.

I did feel a natural urge to serve the nation. I always felt that I should be asking Bapu-ji how to contribute to the betterment of our society. A few days before Bapu-ji's death, one day at eight in the night, I was alone with him in his room. It was freezing cold. He wished to walk a little

and suggested we walk along the length of the room. I
had a few private moments with Bapu-ji then. Scared
that someone would suddenly appear from nowhere and
interrupt our conversation, I decided to ask Bapu-ji about
my life right away. Without wasting a moment I said, 'Bapu-
ji, please tell me, what should I do in life?' I was open to
all his suggestions regarding social service, *khadi* work and
service in the villages.

Bapu-ji was quiet for a couple of moments and then he
said, 'Tara, firstly your mother should be your ideal. Your
father also has plans for you. You have to finish school and
then travel. After you have done all this, then sit and think.
You will find your path.' Through his foresight and wisdom,
Bapu-ji had made his fourteen-year-old granddaughter
aware of her parents' ideas, values and wishes. Not only
did he guide me, he also laid the foundation for the
rest of my life. I had to find my path. Yes, it was a little
upsetting that I was not going to get any relief from going
to school.

We were living the ordinary days of an extraordinary era.
30 January 1948 was just another day in our lives when
it began. I had so much homework to do that I realized it
would be difficult for me to go to Bapu-ji's prayer meeting
that day. I made up my mind not to go for it. Moreover,
Mohan and Ramu also had to study. We thought we would
study more if we stayed at home. It was a freezing winter
day. The idea of staying indoors and eating hot snacks was
also an incentive. I had tea and was about to sit down with
my books when the telephone rang. A voice on the other
end said, 'Mahatma Gandhi has been shot dead.'

Our father was the editor of a newspaper so we were
used to receiving all kinds of news all the time. But this bit

of news seemed so bizarre that I just put the phone down. But it rang again and again and again. It was the same news repeatedly. God knows how my parents heard the news and reached Birla House. When the phone calls became incessant, I picked up Gopu and went out. I don't remember who I went to Birla House with. We had to cut through a huge crowd. The main door was shut. For the first and the only time I loudly proclaimed my relation to Bapu-ji: 'I am Bapu-ji's granddaughter, and this child is my younger brother. Please open the door. I am his granddaughter!' I knocked loud and hard. I don't remember when Mohan and Ramu reached there.

Outside, there was a massive crowd. In Bapu-ji's room, near his body, sat a stunned Pandit Nehru. Manu Behen and Abha Bhabhi seemed numb. Mother was in shock. 'Taru, pay your respects to Bapu-ji,' Father said to me amidst sobs. I had never seen him cry. I kept feeling that Bapu-ji would wake up any minute.

The world was shaken by the death of Mahatma Gandhi. Six decades later, today, human violence and vileness are a scary reality, but Gandhi's land rests on the bedrock of truth, love and non-violence. This truth, love and non-violence still lie in the hearts of the people who bring glory to the country. No books shall be written about these glorious people, neither today nor in the future. But these people work with honesty and dignity in every job they do, and uphold the traditions of the country.

Mohandas Karamchand Gandhi's daily life and routine were steeped in the teachings and philosophies of all our religious texts. He preached them and practised them too.

Birla House is now known as Gandhi Smriti or Gandhi Memorial. Albuquerque Road is now 30 January Road. In this holy place, from the window of my office at the Gandhi Smriti, I can see the constant movement of people from the world over. I also bow, along with nameless citizens of the world, to the Gandhian values of truth and non-violence. I also keep up the tireless search for my own truth.

Lakshmi Devadas Gandhi with daughter Tara, 1935

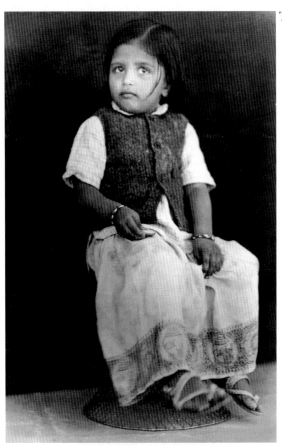

Tara Gandhi, 1936

Tara and Rajmohan, 1939

Rajaji with son
C.R.Narasimhan,Tara and
Rajmohan, 1936

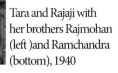

Tara and Rajaji with
her brothers Rajmohan
(left)and Ramchandra
(bottom), 1940

From left to right: Tara, Rajmohan, Ramchandra
and Gopalkrishna c 1947

Mahatma Gandhi and Tara,1947

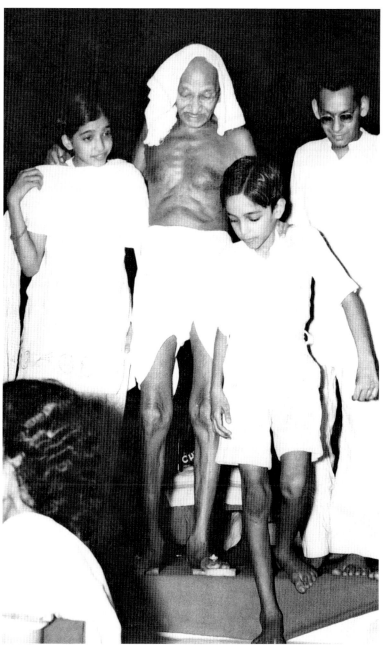

Mahatma Gandhi with Ramchandra and Tara, 1947

From left to right : Lakshmi, Gopalkrishna, Rajaji, Rajmohan, Srimati
Namagiri(elder sister of Lakshmi's) and Tara at Rashtrapati Bhavan,1948

Lakshmi, Gopalkrishna, Tara and leading Indian actor,
Raj Kapoor in Delhi, 1952

A young Tara Gandhi

Tara with friends at Shantiniketan in 1956

Tara with Indira(cousin from her mother's side) before a tennis match in the grounds of Rashtrapati Bhawan, 1948

Pandit Nehru and Rajaji with Tara at her wedding in New Delhi, 1957

Tara and Rajmohan with
parents in London, 1956

Tara at her wedding with philosopher and statesman
Dr. S. Radhakrishnan sitting on the side

Tara and Jyoti at their wedding in New Delhi, 1957

Tara and Jyoti at their wedding reception in New Delhi, 1957

Tara and Jyoti with Srimati Namagiri at their wedding
in New Delhi, 1957

Tara and Jyoti with Sukanya c 1961 in New Delhi

Tara and Jyoti with an Indian delegation visiting Pope Paul VI in the Vatican, 1968. Tara's uncle C.R. Narasimhan is on the left.

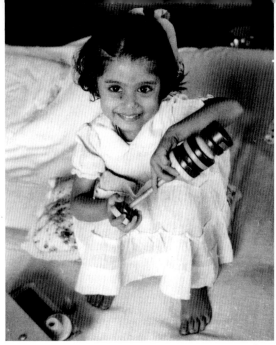

Sukanya, 1962

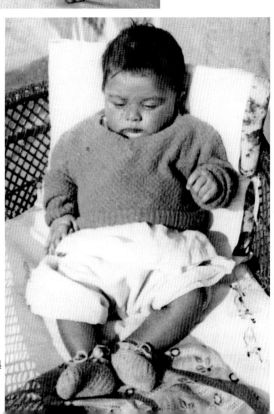

Vinayak , 1964

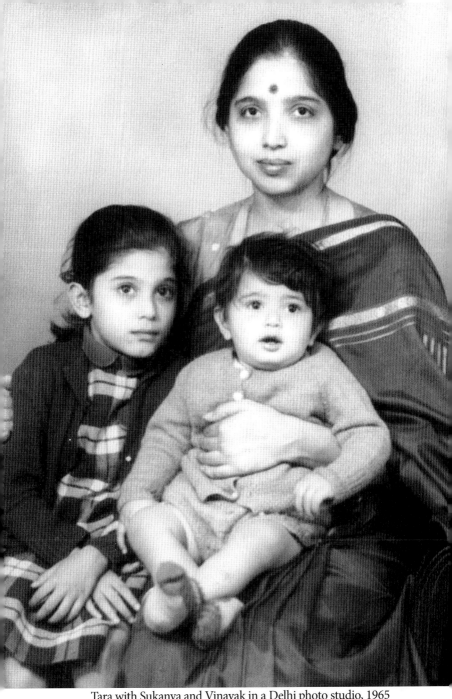

Tara with Sukanya and Vinayak in a Delhi photo studio, 1965

Tara with Sukanya and Pandit Nehru

Tara with her mother Lakshmi holding Sukanya in New Delhi, 1959

Jyoti with colleagues at the Agricultural Institute he founded in
Shantiniketan, West Bengal, 1956

Tara with Rajaji, 1963

Rajaji with Tara and her husband Jyoti Prasad Bhattacharjee
in Moti Bagh residential area, New Delhi, 1963

Rajaji carrying Sukanya, with his son Narasimhan in the
background, 1963

Tara and Jyoti arriving at a reception in Rome, 1969

Jyoti Prasad Bhattacharjee
in Rome, 1976

Jyoti, Tara and Sukanya at a reception in Italy,1968

Tara Bhattacharjee in
Rome, 1976

Jyoti Prasad Bhattachajee
on the terrace of his
home in Bhatpara,
West Bengal, 1981

Construction of Tara's and Jyoti's home in New Delhi, 1981

Sukanya's wedding to Vivek Bharat Ram in November 1986, New Delhi

Tara's sister-in-law Santvana Bhattacharjee, 1998

Santvana (seated on the left) with Vinayak's eldest
daughter Ananya and a relative

From left to right: Santvana, Anoushka, Louise,
Sambhu, Andrea, Ananya, 2004

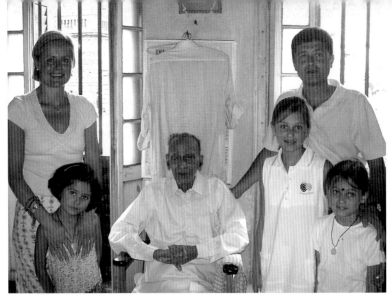

Vinayak, his wife and their children with Sambhu
in Bhatpara, 2004

Clockwise: Sukanya, Vinayak's daughter Ananya, Sukanya's son Vidur, her
husband Vivek Bharat Ram, Vinayak's wife Louise , and Vinayak
Seated from the right: Vivek's mother, Vinayak's daughter Anoushka, Tara,
Vinayak's daughter Andrea, and Vivek's father Dr. Bharat Ram in New Delhi, 2003

Tara with her doll collection, New Delhi, 2010

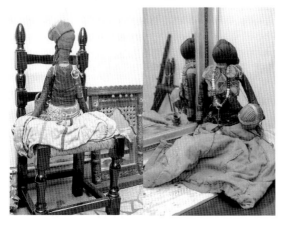

Tara in 2012. Photograph taken by Tiziana Luxardo

Harilal Kaka, Manilal Kaka, Ramdas Kaka

❦

Aesthetics were an integral part of Bapu-ji's life, and his sons were not untouched by its influence. Today I find Bapu-ji's aesthetics reflected in my memories of my father and my uncles – Harilal Kaka, Manilal Kaka and Ramdas Kaka. During Bapu-ji's lifetime, despite my young age, even I did not remain unaffected by Bapu-ji's refined aesthetics, but I do feel that I could have learnt more.

All the brothers looked resplendent in *khadi* dhoti-kurta. In my memories of my uncles, there are many things that seem mundane, yet they are never far from my thoughts. When Manilal Kaka would come home, Mother would always say while making his bed that he liked it clean and white. I understood his nature by seeing how carefully Mother would lay out his bed with a *khadi* sheet and the pillows she chose. Susheela Kaki (his wife) used to say that she had to be extra careful about his food. When Susheela Kaki would come to visit us from South Africa, she would cook Kaka's favourite dishes. What charmed us most about

Kaka was his sense of enjoyment and merriment. When Bapu-ji was leaving South Africa he had ordered his second born, Manilal, to stay there, partly in order to continue his work of Satyagrah and non-violence and partly because he felt a sense of responsibility towards that country. Manilal Kaka spent his entire life there with his family.

Away from his parents, brothers, his country, striving constantly, Manilal Kaka never complained against fate or his father. His sacrifice was extraordinary in the face of his father's challenge. Today I realize how unaffected and simple his nature was. Susheela Kaki would tell us about the class discrimination and its difficulties in South Africa.

Their daughter Sita would tell us stories about life in South Africa. 'It is a beautiful country, but because of the rampant discrimination, there is a big divide in society. So much so that you can't sit on any bench or chair of your choice in a public place.' Sita said.

'What if it is an elderly person, someone who is ill or a child who wishes to sit on a bench in the park?' I asked.

'There is no answer to that question,' Sita answered. 'We just have to assume that there is no facility to sit there. We can be severely punished for using facilities that belong to other class or caste.' Her voice was realistic and not censorious. 'Our schools, hospitals, houses etc. are marked separately. There is a separate division for the Chinese as well. We are kept separated from the blacks as well. Indians are considered brown, dark-skinned. Everyone stays in their own divisions. But you shouldn't get upset about these things.'

'You come there and stay with us. You'll really enjoy the natural beauty,' Kaki would say.

'No Kaki,' I would say. 'I don't want to go there. I will

learn hatred there. I will start to hate the Whites.' Maybe she laughed at my simplicity.

Susheela Kaki would try to teach us Gandhian thought. 'All the children in Bapu-ji's family should know how to spin the *charkha*,' she once told Mother very seriously. 'I will teach Tara and Mohan how to spin *khadi*.' She started by teaching us with spindles of pure cotton. We destroyed so much cotton that Mother could not bear it. 'Bhabhi, why are you wasting such good cotton in trying to teach them?' she said to Kaki.

'If we think of the wastage, the children will never learn how to use the *charkha*,' Kaki replied. Mohan and I kept trying for days. Until we managed to spin a clean thread, Kaki kept us at it for two hours every day. After that, I tried to make spinning a regular part of my daily routine, but was never successful. Even today whenever I spin yarn, I think of Kaki.

Manilal Kaka spent his life away from family and friends in an alien land where his only reality in the social and political set-up was discrimination. In this bitter environment of discrimination and differentiation, Manilal Kaka's nature did not let him become cynical. He exuded positivism all the time.

Ramdas Kaka was an extraordinary person. I always think of him standing tall in his *khadi* kurta and well-tied dhoti that reached down to his ankles. Soft-spoken and gentle, he never lost sight of his goals. He was a stickler for Gandhian principles, and you could see his love for his parents very clearly.

We spent a longer time with Ramdas Kaka, and taking advantage of this proximity, I had long conversations with him. We spoke of his childhood, the time he spent with his parents, and his own philosophy. In fact, I could have learnt much more from Ramdas Kaka about his life, his brothers' lives, about my grandparents from his perspective, the story of a whole era... But I didn't. I was thirty-two or thirty-three years old when he died. I remained ignorant. I hope that his children and my siblings take advantage of Kaka's autobiography and learn more.

Ramdas Kaka's wife, Nirmala Kaki, was a big influence on my life and thoughts. She had internalized Gandhian philosophy and her simplicity and courage fascinated me. Her beauty and the maternal affection she exuded even at ninety years of age were tremendous. After my mother's death, I used to address Kaki as 'Ba'.

Gandhi and Kasturba's eldest daughter-in-law, Harilal Kaka's wife Gulab Kaki, had passed away a long time ago. Farther would remember his eldest sister-in-law with a lot of affection. Harilal Kaka's children, our cousins Kanti, Rami and Manu, were affectionate and a reflection of their mother's warm nature. Kaka's son Rasik had passed away in the prime of his youth. He had been very close to my father and he would always get very emotional remembering his nephew.

Gandhi and Kasturba's sons Manilal, Ramdas and Devadas (my father) worshipped their parents. The eldest, Harilal, was different from the others. He was an enigma to the entire family, and often an adversary of his father. The son's questions, logic and opposition would leave the father speechless. I am sure his paternal affection must have taken a beating for a while. Gandhi's truth had always been his spiritual strength.

Despite being familiar with his father's philosophy of Satyagrah, Harilal never ran out of doubts and queries.

They both had the same objective: to fight and oppose injustice. Harilal's questions to his father in the context of Gandhi's experiments with truth were: 'When I get a chance to go abroad for studies, why do you send others in place of your sons?' and 'We have learnt to spin yarn, fast and go to jail. What job will we get with these qualifications?'

In Gandhi's experiments with truth, in fate, lies his son Harilal's truth as well. Gandhi, in his heart, understood and accepted his son's opposition. Harilal also, in his heart, saluted his father's beliefs. But Harilal Gandhi, in the conviction of his own beliefs, never accepted Bapu-ji's truth for reasons of impracticality in daily life.

Harilal Kaka was also lean like Bapu-ji. He was good looking. He would land up in our house without any prior intimation. We used to love having him over. My mother would lay a clean white neat bed only for a few special people. Amongst these few special people were my maternal grandfather C. Rajagopalachari, Badshah Abdul Ghaffar Khan and my uncles, Harilal Kaka, Manilal Kaka and Ramdas Kaka.

It was a joy to have Harilal Kaka at home. He used to enjoy eating with us and with his brothers. His presence in the house would provide us with a sense of security, which would at times be shadowed by the feeling that just as he had come unannounced, he would leave, too.

Children perceive the said and the unsaid. Though a free spirit, Harilal Kaka was always decorous. In that decorum, there was courage and there was faith. It was his nature that despite being the most familiar with Gandhian thought, he never expressed his opinions about it. Despite understanding the reality of the basic values of the freedom movement, he was not excited by the joy of victory, and nor did he think of himself as pitiful.

Harilal Kaka would talk of routine matters in a good-humoured way. He would draw our attention to the importance of physical exercise. He used to wash his clothes himself with great care and effort. It used to be a spectacle for us to watch him use the least possible amount of soap and water and ensure that the *khadi* shone white. This was also a Gandhian custom – to find enjoyment in learning. Harilal Kaka had left for Delhi immediately on hearing the news of 30 January 1948. It took him two to three days by train from Bombay (now Mumbai). The morning he reached, I was at home with Gopu and my cousin Sumi. Everyone else had gone to Rajghat. 'Kaka, you're a bit late,' I told him. 'The cremation is over.'

'I did not have the right to perform the last rites. That right belongs to your fathers,' he said to Sumi and me.

It was a sunny winter day. Kaka washed his clothes and was drying them on the terrace. I picked up the clothes to help him. 'Drying them out is an important part of the process of washing clothes. If they are not hung out properly to dry they are wasted,' Kaka explained to me as I helped him. 'See, you should pull both ends of the dhoti and kurta properly when you hang them out. They dry faster and don't need to be ironed. Of course, you have to fold them well too.' Even today, while washing and drying clothes, I invariably think of Harilal Kaka. When the whole world was in mourning, when the country was trying to come to terms with the brutal reality of Gandhi's sacrifice, and Rajghat resonated with prayers of the last rites, Gandhi's eldest son was teaching his niece how to wash clothes. Harilal Kaka did not express in words how he had integrated Gandhi's life and his Satyagrah into his own life. But the sound of Kaka's thoughts touched a fourteen-year-old girl. 'Long live Bapu. You are great, Bapu.'

When Kaka told Sumi and me that the right to perform Bapu-ji's last rites belonged to our fathers, he did not say this with any ill will towards anybody nor in self-deprecation. It was the culmination of his belief and his courage. These were extraordinary values and affirmations in the exceptionally virtuous experiments of mankind, whose foundation was built on the ordinary yet sincere values of a son.

Essays by Tara Gandhi Bhattacharjee

*Women as Victims in Conflict Areas and
as Promoters of Peace*

*

Charkha: The Hand Spinning Wheel

*

A Story about Dolls

*

The Meaning of Swaraj

Women as Victims in Conflict Areas and as Promoters of Peace

❧

The Earth is mother Goddess. The River Ganges is Goddess Mother. Saraswati is the Goddess of learning and wisdom. The creation is mother. *Shakti* – strength – is mother. Goddess Durga is the protector of all life. Goddess Kali is the destroyer of all evil. They are the symbols of strength and their virtues are inherent in the being of a woman.

As a bit of contradiction, it is interesting to note that the women of India in general, consciously or unconsciously, are also conditioned by those mythological women who display immense courage in the face of the established conventions of society. Draupadi, of the epic Mahabharata, was married to the five Pandava brothers, but to this day, she remains the symbol of spiritual strength, truth, love and justice.

Kunti, again from the Mahabharata, is a fascinating character, who was secretly in love with Surya – the Sun God – had a son from Him, before and apart from her three other sons from her husband. These unconventional women from mythology are indeed very admirable. I find it very interesting to note the strong unconventional streaks of influence in the so-called conservative and traditional Indian women. I am, of course, speaking on the basis of my context. But I feel that these could be the characteristics of women everywhere.

While conscious of the spiritual sparks in her being, a woman is equally conscious of her sense of logic and action on a practical level. She is physically less powerful than a man, but her biological vulnerability, her ability to be a mother, is what also transforms in her supreme strength. The animal instinct of protecting one's offspring can reach the highest and sublimest level in a woman. She has the natural inner force to transform her maternal love into care for the entire society. Even in the state of war, terror or in a crisis, a wailing, weeping woman pushes aside her sorrow to realize the responsibility of a protector, a sister, a daughter, a friend and a mother. A liberated woman is not necessarily a professional, working and intellectual woman. She could be a home manager too.

Talking to an Italian woman in Rome in 1931, Mahatma Gandhi had said: 'The beauty of a non-violent war is that women can play the same part in it as men. Indian women played a more effective part in our last non-violent war than men. The reason is simple: A non-violent war calls into play suffering to the largest extent. And who can suffer more purely and nobly than women? The women in India tore away the *purdah* and came forward to work for the nation. They saw that the country demanded something more than their looking after their homes. They manufactured contraband salt, they picketed foreign-cloth shops and liquor shops, and tried to wean both the seller and the customer from both. At late hours in the night, they pursued the drunkards to their dens with courage and charity in their hearts. They marched to jails and they sustained *lathi* (wooden sticks) blows as few men did. If the women of the West will try to vie with men in becoming brutes, they have no lesson to learn from the women of India. They will have to cease to take delight in sending their husbands and sons to kill people and congratulate them on their valour. To quote Ralph Emerson 'There is no evil worse than a bad woman, and nothing has ever been produced better than a good one.'

The Kasturba Gandhi National Memorial Trust (KGNMT) was founded by Mahatma Gandhi before the independence of India to honour the memory of Kasturba who died in the year 1944. Mahatma Gandhi said Kasturba Trust would have a bigger place in a free India. For, all would go to the winds, if the women were not properly trained. He hoped that every worker in the Trust would have a great deal to give to the new government.

In Gandhi's words, 'we must generate that strength within us. We must not be frightened of making mistakes. Man is born to make mistakes, but the great thing is to identify our mistakes and learn from them. We should magnify our own errors so as to be deterred from committing them again. Those who imagine that they never make mistakes are to be feared.'

He agreed with one of the members when she said that it was a great tragedy that the uplift of women had to be an item on the constructive agenda. 'Have we yet to find ourselves?' she asked. The reply was: Yes, indeed, and how better can you find yourselves than by being true to the highest traditions of Indian women and by serving your unhappy sisters today?'

One worker asked that while he did not advocate their taking any part in politics, what would he advise them to do in case of violent outbreaks?

Mahatma Gandhi answered: 'There is no question of any of your keeping aloof from the fiery furnace, should it ever come your way. I shall not shed a tear.'

For more than 64 years now, the Trust and all its branches in each state of India have been incessantly working for the cause of needy women and children of rural India. Distinguished and selfless women and men have guided this Trust. It has set an unparalleled example of reaching out to help the needy in the society in times of natural and man-made disasters and terrors.

Talking of the courage of a woman, my mind takes me back to my meeting with Helen Keller of America. She was in her 50s or 60s; I was in college then. My parents had taken me to meet her. The tall, heavy and gentle lady emanating wisdom and sensitivity around her was a special guest of Prime Minister Nehru in India. Helen Keller could not see, hear or talk. Her words and fingers were very sensitive. She reacted with touch.

Through her interpreter, she was explaining her joy at seeing India and realizing the beauty of India in her soul. She said she could feel the colours of flowers in their perfume. Through touch and smell, she described the beauty and goodness of people. She smiled like a young child. She sensed the sensitivity of the next person. She was an ardent admirer of Bapu and Pandit Nehru and the peace loving leaders of the world. Helen Keller's life and message will remain a source of strength to the society always. As Elizabeth C. Stanton Pope said, 'Social science affirms that a woman's place in a society marks the level of its civilization.'

In 1947, Mahatma Gandhi wrote to Chinese women, 'If only the women of the world would come together they could display such heroic non-violence as to kick away the atom bomb like a mere ball. Women have been so gifted by God... If an ancestral treasure lying buried in a corner of the house unknown to the members of the family were suddenly discovered, what a celebration it would occasion! Similarly women's marvelous power is lying dormant. If the women of Asia wake up, they will dazzle the world. My experiment in non-violence would be instantly successful if I could secure women's help.'

'As soldiers of peace, women have shown a heroic fortitude fully equal to that of men,' said Lao Tsu.

I want to tell you the story of a little girl in Bangladesh. I went to Bangladesh for the first time some years ago. An activist woman writer was my host there. From Dacca, we were to cross the river Meghna in a ferry to get to the other side. Our car drove us right on to the ferry from where we entered a noisy and colourful bazaar bustling with life. People were selling, buying and eating. There were fakirs and philosophers, cycles, cycle-rikshaws, small and heavy motor vehicles.

It was a complete picture of Bangladesh, in all its colours and sounds, and with the scents from the Meghna river flowing on both sides of the ferry. All of a sudden, I noticed a young girl of about 14 years, offering water from a jug to the travellers. She had a completely worn sari wrapped around her and was barefoot. What attracted me most about her was her vivacious personality and her beautiful black eyes. I found her staring at me. Then she came near me and looked at me with a mischievous smile.

'Do you want water?' she asked.

I said, 'No, I do not want water. But I want to give you something.'

'No please, No–' she cried. 'I do get money because I serve water. But I do not want money or anything else from you.'

She was so interesting. I asked what her name was.

'Fatima,' she said.

'Why are you staring at me?' I asked.

'I like your *Bindi*. I like your bracelets. You are a foreigner.'

She was getting more and more interesting. 'I speak your language. Many women here also wear a *bindi* and bracelets. How do you make out that I am a foreigner?'

'I don't know,' she said. 'But I like you. You are a guest and I will not take any money from you.'

'Where do you live?' I asked.

'I live there in that village,' she pointed to a far off village on the other bank of the river.

'My younger brother and I live there with my grandmother. My grandmother works with a weaver to make the hand-woven cloth. It is my responsibility to see my younger brother educated. There is no one else in the family.'

I was shaken. Fatima appeared as a symbol of abject poverty and her grandmother as one of the many who live in poverty but keep people like me so honoured in hand-spun clothes. Fatima's younger brother, a hope to her future, sounded like a challenge to the conscience of all humanity.

I was fighting my thoughts when Fatima held my hand and said smilingly, 'I want to take you to my hut on the other side of the river.'

'O Fatima, I will definitely come, but on my way back...' I said. She asked the date and time of my return to the ferry from the other side. Then she smiled with joy: 'A promise?'

'Yes, a promise,' I said.

Then she was quiet for a while. What will I give you to eat in my house? I could read her thoughts.

'Fatima, I do not eat fish, I do not eat rice, I cannot eat sweets. But can you give me puffed dry rice?' I am very fond of *Muri*. I love *Muri* and puffed dry rice.

She gave a broad smile. We also love to eat *Muri*. We will all eat *Muri* then.

Puffed dry rice is the poorest person's snack and is also a substitute for a proper meal.

The ferry was reaching the shore and Fatima waved her hands saying, 'It is my promise and your promise too. My grandmother will be very happy to hear that you are coming.'

She did not know anything about me. She just knew I was a foreigner and she liked me.

After a few hectic but exciting days, we were to return from the same ferry. I was thinking of all the lovely people we had left behind. My mind was full of all the experiences I had had. When our car was driving on to the ferry, a boy came running to my car and said, 'Are you the foreigner who was invited by my sister Fatima to visit our home?'

'Yes, how is Fatima?' I did not want Fatima to be compelled to keep that promise to me, which was made by her in an impulsive way.

'I am happy to meet you,' I said.

'I have also been waiting to meet you,' the boy said. 'My sister had described you so well that I could recognize you in an instant.'

'I want to visit your house. Please show me the way.' I requested the driver to stop and turn for Fatima's village.

'No,' the boy said, 'we will not be able to receive you today.'

The boy had an urgent message. 'Our grandmother died this morning and Fatima is with the body. She has sent me to inform you of this situation. We are very sorry that we cannot receive you today.'

I was speechless, my voice choked. I tried to say something and the boy nodded, as though to say that he understood my shock and sorrow at the sad news, but he was in a great haste to rush back.

I had not taken my promise seriously, but Fatima had and with pure responsibility. Fatima had the presence of mind and the alertness to keep her word in the midst of a tragedy that fell like lightening on her and her younger brother. Fatima was not a symbol of poverty anymore for me. She was the soul of Bangladesh to me and also the symbol of human integrity. I myself had become a symbol of moral poverty, helplessness and inactivity. Why did I not visit Fatima's house and offer some help? My host suggested, 'Fatima represents the soul of our nation.'

Fatima certainly is the soul of humanity. The child is the future father and the future mother. The responsibility of the mother in a woman and the father in a man is to leave a beautiful memory of love and compassion in her/his child for the world of tomorrow.

Charkha
The Hand Spinning Wheel

∽∾

In India the cloth spun and woven by hand is called *khadi* or *khaddar*.

Representing philosophy, beauty and reality, the hand spinning wheel called *charkha* was the most potent tool of non-violence and of the *satyagraha* led by Mahatma Gandhi. The *charkha* became the symbol of the Indian freedom movement. The handspun, hand-woven cloth and the hand spinning wheel, heritage of humanity through the ages, were reborn in India as an inseparable part of Bapu's life and philosophy.

Woven to create exquisite fabrics, textures, and designs in silk, wool and cotton, the handspun threads of the hand spinning wheel are a source of employment to millions of men and women in rural India today. The *charkha*'s threads represent the flow of the eternal threads of creation – threads of love and peace.

The above definition of *khadi* is neither profound nor complete. It is not defined by an academician; it has emerged from a sincere heart that is involved with the integral nature of *khadi* where the threads of the spinning wheel weave the warp and weft of the fabric of our society.

The threads of the *charkha* have unfolded to me the meaning of life and creation. In the Persian language, I am told that *charkha* means the 'sky' or 'space'. The word *khadi* may be a derivative of *'khaddi'*, the trench or hollow in the ground under the loom. There is a non-dualism about it that makes me relate it to the cosmic flow.

With homage to the Sufi philosophy of saint-poet Kabir, I see my life as a continuous patchwork of all colours and forms of time and space. The threads of the patches and the thread that joins them are the threads of that spinning wheel, which has spun my life. The sound of the spinning wheel becomes the sound of my soul when I wonder about the soundlessness beyond vision and timelessness beyond space.

My journey with the spinning wheel must have started before my birth, but neither can this journey ever be complete, nor can it be defined; just as the threads of the warp and the weft of the cloth are endless. I know for certain that I would fail miserably in a Gandhian test of *khadi*. Yet, the romance of my life with the journey of *khadi* has brought to me revelations that have enabled me to understand the truth and force of Mahatma Gandhi's thoughts and actions.

Khadi as a concept and as a reality has mind, body and soul. It is an inseparable part of the Indian ethos. But this human and spiritual reality does not belong to India alone. Cloth was one of man's first encounters with civilization. Leather, tree bark, wool, silk and cotton all provided material and clothing to man.

Until industrialization and the advent of machines, all cloth all over the world was *khadi* by definition. It was hand spinning and hand weaving that provided man with every kind of texture and material.

Ironically when the Industrial Revolution caused the world to drift away from this supreme handicraft, there was a revival and renaissance of the hand spinning wheel in India. The philosophy of *satyagraha* was revealed to Mohandas Karamchand Gandhi in South Africa. But India gave him the vision of the philosophy of *charkha*. South Africa was the inspiration and action ground of Mahatma Gandhi for more than two decades before he conceived the potential of the hand spinning wheel in India as the atom bomb of non-violence. As the symbol of economic, political and social reality of India, the *charkha* manifested itself as the message of non-violence.

The tiniest *takli* – the spindle – became the most potent tool in Gandhi's non-violent battle of *satyagraha*. The music of the *charkha* unfolded the meaning of *satyagraha* to the people of India. As the message of *sarvodaya,* the way to *swaraj* (self-rule), and the thread of *swadeshi* (self-made) and *swavalamban* (self-reliance), the spinning wheel united the country. The English were threatened and weakened by the sound of the *charkha*'s simple and universal wheel.

At Bapu's call, the export of Indian cotton to England was to be stopped. There was no need for Indians to buy expensive imported cloth made from their own cotton. The *charkha* was a means of non-violently undermining foreign rule. Uniting people politically and socially and bringing dignity to manual labour, as a symbol of total self-rule, the *charkha* also became a meditational therapy of its own kind. Inspired by the example set by Bapu, Pandit Nehru and other stalwarts of the era, the non-violent fighters for India's freedom began spinning *khadi* in prisons, during prayer meetings and during political rallies. They would spin on trains and in the ashrams. A delicate thread strongly bound together a nascent nation.

The philosophy of *charkha* and Mahatma Gandhi was inseparable from *satyagraha* and *sarvodaya*. Mahatma Gandhi was inspired by the concept of *sarvodaya* while reading the book *Unto this Last* by John Ruskin on a train journey from Johannesburg to Durban. *Sarvodaya* is the reawakening of the spirit in harmony with nature and environment, and for all forms of life. Political liberation was only the first step. The spinning wheel, with the message of *swadeshi*, was to lead us to a reconstruction of the social and economic order, without the exploitation of man and nature. Total *swaraj* was a vision of *sarvodaya*. To quote Mahatma Gandhi, 'The weaver of the *khadi* from a *swadeshi* standpoint is like a man making use of his lungs.

Mahatma Gandhi explains, '*Khadi* is the occupation that will give employment to millions... I can instil my faith in the potency of hand-spinning in the minds of the toilers of India not by making speeches but by spinning myself' – (*Young India*, May 20, 1926)

'*Khadi* has no established market like that of mill cloth. It has not even become as yet a bazaar article. Every yard of *khadi* bought means at least 80 per cent of its price in the mouths of the starving and the poor of India. Every yard of mill cloth bought means more than 75 per cent of its price in the pockets of the capitalists and less than 25 per cent in the pockets of the labourers who are never helpless, who are well able to take care of themselves, and who never starve or need starve in the sense that the helpless millions starve for whose sake *khadi* has been conceived' – (*Young India*, October 4, 1928)

The following are some of Mahatma Gandhi's important points on *khadi* and the spinning wheel:

- Learn spinning yourself whether for recreation or for maintenance.
- Learn weaving yourself whether for recreation or for maintenance.
- Spinning supplies the readiest occupation to those who have leisure and are in want of a few coppers.
- Spinning is known to the thousands.
- Spinning is easily learnt.
- Spinning requires practically no outlay of capital.
- The wheel can be easily and cheaply made. Most of us do not yet know that spinning can be done even with a piece of tile and splinter.
- The people have no repugnance to it.
- It affords immediate relief in times of famine and scarcity.
- It alone can stop the drain of wealth from India through the purchase of foreign cloth.
- It automatically distributes the millions thus saved among the deserving poor.
- Even the smallest success means so much immediate gain to the people.
- It is the most potent instrument of securing cooperation among the people.

What is the reality of *khadi* today after 64 years of India's political independence? Where is the vision of *sarvodaya* today? According to Mahatma Gandhi, God appears in the form of food for the hungry millions. Has *khadi* reached out to them? While mirroring all the contradictions of our society and country, the despair and vulgarity, as well as the hope of the strength and beauty of India – the *khadi* world today represents the continuous degeneration and mismanagement of the political and social scene of India today. Unfortunately the lack of individual and collective responsibility has resulted in the outrageous reality of present-day India and present-day *khadi*.

Politics, the government, the Gandhian *khadi* institutions, and the people are all responsible for this degeneration. Instead of setting an inspirational, dynamic example for the government, politics and society, the Gandhian and *khadi* institutions have become badly run organizations dependent on government subsidies and patronage for survival.

The welfare of the spinners and the weavers and the self-reliance of the *khadi* institutions are the real spirit of *khadi*. That spirit is lost somewhere now. *Khadi* depends on the spinners and the weavers for both its production and meaning. Nothing can be achieved in the *khadi* sector without the aim of reaching the welfare of the spinners and weavers. The makers of *khadi* are the artists of this beautiful fabric. These makers are exploited, the real spirit and intrinsic foundation of *khadi* are lost.

My journey with *khadi* has brought me very close to some stark realities in the world of *khadi* and *gramodyog,* village industry. It has also given me great moments of exhilaration.

Khadi and *gramodyog* have the potential to restore grace and dignity to the lives of millions of people who, so far, are, without any bitterness and violence and who also don't seem to have great ambition. But, without vision and leadership these people may lose their dignity and hope and give way to violence. Some beautiful Himalayan areas like Sikkim have revealed to me the need for some unifying indigenous activist agent such as *khadi*.

Khadi and *gramodyog* can also reach out to forgotten areas like the islands of Andaman and Nicobar. I was amazed to see the great, so far untapped, potential for ayurvedic medicines and vegetable dyes as well as the possibilities of developing several other village industries, without damaging and polluting the pure atmosphere and nature of the most historic islands of the world.

I must mention the Victoria and Albert Museum in London that has an incredibly huge collection of fabulous materials – wool, silk and cotton – from all parts of India in the 16th–18th centuries. Gorgeous handspun and hand-woven *pashminas, jamawars* and exquisite weaves in silk and cotton were continuously being loaded on to ships sailing from India to England for sale, exhibition and royal possession. Today after a few centuries, we can be grateful at least for the superb preservation of our priceless heritage that almost vibrates with the sound and sentiments of its time, its land, and its people.

Over the centuries, art and tradition have retained the same flow in India, but challenges keep meeting us at every turn. Degeneration is unceasing in the quality of life for our supreme artists.

The handspun and hand-woven tradition and the art of the historic and world famous muslin of Bengal continues in Nabadwip and Murshidabad. The purest tradition of spinning and weaving of Ponduru in Andhra Pradesh creates exclusive and beautiful *khadi* that is the supremely coveted and cherished possession of all its wearers. But the artists of Ponduru and the artists of the Bengal muslin are often the landless poor who are paid appallingly low daily wages for their art.

The art of Sambalpur is also very revealing and challenging. The weave of Sambalpur is a priceless expression of the supreme handicraft that is *khadi*. But the spinners and the weavers of Orissa have remained the poorest in the country.

The whole situation leads one to study the intricate psychology involved in artistic production and consumerism. The first producer was also his own consumer. Man originally made his own tools, his cooking utensils, his furniture and his clothes for his basic needs. In other words, the consumer made items for his need and necessity and then added ornamentation to his creation.

As the society evolved, there were natural, psychological, social and economic reasons to separate the producer and the consumer. Slowly, over a period of time, a producer was not necessarily the consumer and the consumer was not always a producer. The consumer was getting ready to pay a higher price to satisfy his needs and aesthetic sense.

But, what happens when for centuries, generations of producers create objects of aesthetic value for which consumers cannot afford to pay a price commensurate with the labour and creativity involved? The society enjoys a rich aesthetic heritage without paying the price for it. The producers of priceless value remain in poverty as well as in ignorance of the richness of their creation.

I have seen this situation in Orissa, Assam, Bengal, Andhra Pradesh, and in various other parts of the country. The eternal question is how to save this priceless heritage and retain the dignity and grace in the lives of the artists who are continuing this heritage.

Travelling through various regions of the country, I have seen rural people, women and men, spinning cotton wool on a *takli* – a hand spindle – or on a traditional *charkha*, in colourful bazaar squares, in dusty streets, and outside their mud huts. Once I approached a very colourfully attired man spinning on a hand spindle in a village street bazaar in Gujarat. The air in the bazaar was dusty and it was full of the most colourful, happy and noisy village folk. There were camels, gypsies and vendors of all sorts of traditional and local wares – toys, balloons, bangles, cooking pots, etc.

The tall, dark young man intrigued me. He was wearing the regional *dhoti* and *kediyum* – the traditional Gujarati *kurta* for men, a hand-woven *chaddar* (wrap), and of course, the *bandhani* turban. Add to this, his moustache and the golden round earrings and he was definitely the model of the village heroes of our films. He was relishing a gossip with a group of similar looking men. He stood out for his simultaneous flawless spinning. I interrupted their conversation and asked this young man in Gujarati:

'Excuse me, brother, can I ask you a question?'

He looked at me with surprise that he wanted to hide. There was a twinkle in his eyes. 'Yes?' he said. The men around him were also curious about this encounter.

'Are you spinning for *khadi*?' I asked.

'What do you mean by *khadi*?' he said.

'I mean *khadi* where the thread is spun by hand and woven by hand.' I was surprised he did not know about *khadi* and could not relate it to hand-spinning. 'I mean this,' I said, touching his spindle.

'Oh, I am spinning for my *chaddar*. I will give it to a friend and he will weave it for me.

'Will he weave it by hand?' I asked.

'Yes, this is how we make our clothes and *chaddar*. Maybe you are new here and not familiar with our traditions.'

'But you did not understand when I said *khadi*,' I argued.

'*Khadi*? What is that?'

The spectators were curious but they got bored by our conversation. The young man had sympathy for my ignorance. But they could not believe that someone could be that ignorant about the most natural tradition of spinning thread, and I could not believe that someone who spun by hand did not understand the word *khadi*.

Similar experiences in various parts of the country made me realize that the nameless flow of the thread of the spinning wheel is the inherent flow of our ethos and reality.

My cook from the hills in Uttaranchal once asked me about spinning, 'Why do you need so many kinds of *charkha*? We in our village break a small, hooked twig from a tree and use it as a spindle to spin wool.' He was unconsciously describing the original *takli*.

It was from this nameless, consistent and gracious flow of the spinning wheel that the *khadi* movement could emerge with the renaissance of the *charkha*, for the political freedom of the country and beyond, towards the vision of *sarvodaya*.

After Independence, the organized *khadi* and village industries were supported and subsidized by the government. This was aimed at creating gainful employment for the needy millions across the country, so that way beyond the shrieks and roars of heavy industrialization, the threads of *swadeshi* and *swavalamban* could reach the masses with dignity and without exploitation.

But through all the past decades of our political freedom, in spite of great potential and achievements, the flow of *khadi* has taken some ugly turns, reflecting the mood and the state of the country itself.

I am often asked questions like: Is there a degeneration in the *khadi* organizations today? Why don't we get good varieties of *khadi* in the *khadi* outlets, and why are *charkhas* not easily available? Why is *khadi* so expensive? What do you think of the latest experiments of designers with *khadi* and the export of *khadi*?

There is no substitute for Gandhian philosophy and *khadi* in India, However, against the background of stark exploitation of the spinners and the weavers, by what reasoning and measure do we evaluate the marketing of *khadi*? Its life is neglected and exploited at the source; what quality and growth can we expect to emerge from the spinning wheel to the *khadi* outlets in the form of final products?

The lack of availability of various types of traditional *charkha* and *pun* (rolls of treated raw cotton, which are then spun on the spindle) is a serious obstacle. The documentation on *khadi* is also unbelievably lacking. It is not surprising then that the availability of good quality and varieties of *khadi* is a problem. Most often the *khadi* that is available has colours that run. A lot of *khadi* comes damaged, shop-soiled, and even eaten by rats sometimes. Can there be a greater apathy not just to this supreme expression of art but to the poor and needy people who create it?

I have heard some people complain about the lack of modernization and professionalism in *khadi* outlets. What pains me is not the lack of sophistication in *khadi* shops, but that non-*khadi* materials are infiltrating into *khadi* shops and are being sold as pure *khadi*.

I once rejected a sari in a *khadi* shop saying that it was non-*khadi*. I may have sounded very virtuous and self-righteous, but my rejection was not meant as an insult to the makers of that non-*khadi* material. My point was that it was equally insulting to the non-*khadi* material to give it a false banner. If non-*khadi* materials are to be sold in *khadi* shops, they should be sold with their true identity and not as *khadi*. This way, we can be honest to *khadi* as well as non-*khadi*.

What remains almost a miracle is the fact that despite the ignorant and deplorable marketing, exquisite and useful *khadi* remains available and in production.

Then there is the question – why is *khadi* so expensive? In my view, the high price, in today's context, can only be justified provided that this is in the interest of the spinners, the weavers and the artisans. But one is back to the grim reality that the producers receive no benefits from the high price of *khadi*.

Khadi has always honoured me, but I wonder today – what does the *khadi* I wear mean to me? My *khadi* is precious. It is exquisite and comfortable. But I also perceive the whiteness of my *khadi* as a statement in the face of oppression, violence and injustice. My *khadi* also reminds me of the unfriendly, deafening noise of the Ambar *Charkhas* that are operated by emaciated women who are spinning in hot crowded rooms, and whose daily wages are often pending.

Once some very self-righteous *khadi* people were suggesting to a group of spinners that they should be wearing *khadi*. What my *khadi* friends got as an answer from the emaciated women was a speechless, but unconsciously philosophical stare. I felt awkward and guilty in my *khadi*. People who make exquisite cloth for us remain clothless, just as the labourers, who lay bricks for our houses and palaces, remain roofless, and as the farmers, who grow grain for our food, remain hungry.

Khadi is of course as popular as it was during Mahatma Gandhi's time, if not more so. Consumers are wearing *khadi* because of its elegance and because it suits their skin through the various seasons of the year (I am talking of the cotton *khadi* and certainly not of polyester *khadi*). A major difference between Mahatma Gandhi's time and today is that although *khadi* is very popular, consumers do not have much knowledge and information about this handspun and hand-woven cloth, nor are they conscious of its historic and symbolic significance.

The gulf between the producer – the spinner and the weaver – and the consumer is increasing all the time. The very nature of handicraft and its survival requires certain affinity between producer and consumer.

As far as experiments of designing with this fabric are concerned, the handspun and hand-woven cloth in itself is a supreme expression of art. It is not surprising that some leading designers have decided to work with it. *Khadi* cannot be part of industrialized mass production. It is a craft that belongs with exclusive hand production. This fabric that is both handspun and hand-woven should only be exported in a very special and limited way. Once when I presented a small *khadi* towel to an Italian friend, she said that she would not use it as a towel but honour it by framing and hanging it in her drawing room.

The thread of the spinning wheel has introduced me to

friends and strangers in different lands who have inspired me with their enthusiasm and sensitive appreciation of *khadi*. While on a pilgrimage to Bangladesh and Pakistan, I wanted to pay homage to the philosophy and reality of *khadi* in these parts of the Subcontinent, which like India, owe their liberation to the *charkha*. Noakhali in Bangladesh is a testimony of the philosophy of Gandhi and philosophy of *khadi*.

In the beautiful areas of Sindh and the northwest frontier of Pakistan, I came across streams of the real pure flow of *khadi*. *Khadi* is known as *khaddar or khadi ka kapra* in Pakistan. With very limited production, the tradition of *khadi* has survived in these parts. And as it is not supported or sponsored by the State, it has unconsciously adhered to *khadi*'s intrinsic spirit and philosophy. The tall, handsome Pathans of Charsadda are very proud of their coarse *khaddar*. The subject of *khadi* was met with great enthusiasm arid respect by politicians, businessmen and intellectuals in Lahore, Karachi and Islamabad. They all said that there is an urgent need for a continuous exchange of ideas and exhibitions for *khadi* and handicrafts between India and Pakistan. *Khadi* and *gramodyog* brought us together and also made us forget the subject of Kashmir.

My hosts in Karachi kept admiring my saris from Ponduru. I left some Ponduru fabric for them. It was the least I could do to show my appreciation for their extremely warm hospitality. The overwhelming hospitality in Pakistan comes from the elite as well as the poor. The finest thread of *khadi* touched me, as did Pakistan with its warm friendship.

On board a flight in South Africa, I was sitting next to a very elegant young black lady. I smiled at her and was thinking of the right words to start a conversation. Before I could say anything, she said, 'Excuse me, can I touch your dress to feel the texture? It is such an attractive cloth.' 'Of course,' I said happily as I stretched out the end of my sari. She felt the rough texture of the cloth as I observed her beautiful hand adorned with diamond rings. 'This cloth is so beautiful!' she exclaimed. 'I am a Zulu princess and I am getting married next week. I wish I could have material like this for my bridal trousseau.' My sari was made of off-white, thick and coarse *khadi* from Uttar Pradesh. I was surprised that it could appeal so instantly to a Zulu princess. I mentioned to her that I had always been fascinated by the vibrant handicraft and fabrics of Africa. When she said that she had particularly liked the coarseness of my material, I had to explain to her the concept of *khadi*. She was fascinated to hear of the continuity of the tradition of handloom.

People in strange lands have amazed me with their appreciation of this heritage. I was explaining the philosophy of *khadi* to a friend in Uruguay who said, 'It is this message of the spinning wheel that we want to have from India, because it inspires us to honour and revive our own traditions of weaving and other forgotten handicrafts.' He organized a big exhibition called 'The Thread of the Spinning Wheel' in Montevideo.

In India, the simplicity of *khadi* and Gandhian living are often not understood. Shabbiness, ugliness, and even the lack of cleanliness are accepted in the name of simplicity, refinement and beauty. The word 'fashion' applied to the context of *khadi* and Gandhi is almost considered as sacrilege.

I defend the word 'fashion' in the context of *khadi*. Fashion is a mode, a way of life, and an expression of the mind and society, so cloth cannot be dissociated from fashion.

Khadi is cloth. The classical and traditional Indian fashion of attire for men and women, the rich and the poor, has always remained an uncut and untailored length of cloth. *Dhoti, sari, lungi, chaddar*, and *pagri* are all various lengths of cloth. For a weary traveller the *chaddar* can become a rolled pillow, as well as a tent, or even a hammock for a baby.

A group of friends from Europe, who were in India to attend a wedding, had asked me once, 'What should we wear to look Indian?' 'Wear whatever you like,' I said, 'but carry a *chaddar* or *odhani* with you and you will look Indian. You will also define your style by the flair with which you wear the length of cloth.'

Mahatma Gandhi was always experimenting with his clothing in harmony with his philosophy. In the last decades of his life, he wore the uncut length of the short *dhoti* of the Indian farmer. Without any tailored garment, the classical short *dhoti* and the classical *chaddar* gave the message of *satyagraha* and identified Bapu with the simple farmers of the country.

In today's global world, Bapu's supreme guidance is most relevant. He had said that for our economic needs the world is our village, and for our spiritual needs the village is our world. Today, while the spinners and weavers are being exploited, the *khadi* institutions have also subjected themselves to total dependence on the Government in the last six decades. The *khadi* industry should have worked towards self-reliance instead; giving up Government subsidies and rebates today would result in the complete paralysis of the *khadi* institutions. They prefer to depend on financial aid from the Government while themselves exploiting vulnerable spinners and poor artisans.

In the vision of *sarvodava, khadi* cannot be de-linked from other questions like: Are we keeping our environment, our surroundings, our cities and our institutions clean? What are the efforts of the so-called Gandhian towards creating a fearless and violence-free society? The majority of our children are deprived of compassion and love. What is our attitude towards these children who represent our future? Why don't we give them a direction and a vision? How do we stop the message of terror and violence in films and other media? How do we treat animals in our country? There is the horror of increasing violence against women and weaker sections of society – what is our reaction? What is our action against it? Where is the philosophy of *khadi* and what is the reality of *khadi* today?

Human violence and environmental pollution are an everyday reality in India. Yet, India, where individually and collectively we live at thousands of levels, is so full of contradictions that whatever one may say, the exact opposite is also true. If we speak of violence somewhere, the contradiction of violence is also a reality. This paradoxical contradiction of the negative is our hope and our strength, too.

The truth and hope of the *khadi* philosophy is a challenge to our conscience today. We can literally as well is metaphorically say that the weave has got badly tangled in the web of *khadi*. If the clean threads cannot be extricated from the tangled web, fresh threads will have to be spun for a new weave.

The answers and the solutions to the challenges of the philosophy of *sarvodaya* are inherent in the philosophy of *khadi*. When the thread of the *charkha* will reach the poorest woman spinner as her product and as her cloth, the music of the *charkha* and the rhythmic clack of the castanet of the loom will represent the reawakening of the spirit of *sarvodaya*.

There is a direction for us in one of Mahatma Gandhi's talismans:

> *'I will give you a Talisman. Whenever you are in doubt or when the self becomes too much for you, apply the following test: Recall the face of the poorest and the weakest man whom you may have seen and ask yourself if the step you contemplate is going to be of any use to him. Will he gain anything by it? Will it restore him to a control over his own life and destiny? In other words, will it lead to swaraj for the hungry and spiritually starving millions? Then you will find your doubts and your self melting away.'*

A Story about Dolls

Khadi and my dolls have given me a raison d'etre. I can't bear to throw away even an inch of cloth, and older the material the more precious it becomes for me. The only things I buy for my dolls are sewing needle and thread. Even the stuffing is made of old rags. Old buttons, safety pins, curtain rings and strings and several old discarded pieces from the junk box seem so fascinating... I keep using them to add personality to forms, which result from the interplay of colours and cloth. I have not given any name to these creations, but I find complete identifications in their facelessness. Where is the need for more definition?

Playing with dolls as a child, how could I have known that my childhood love for them would, carrying through adolescence and youth, become a symbol of my love for beauty, both inner and outer, in my old age. In my childhood, all foreign-made things were banned in our house. One day my mother's friend got us some very beautiful 'Made in Germany' colour pencils. We'd never seen pencils like those before. Mother told her friend very clearly, 'No, we cannot take this.' In the face of my mother's soft words and firm belief, none of her friend's arguments worked.

But one day, my mother allowed herself to be swept away by her love for me and summoned the courage to buy me a foreign doll. Those were the days of the national movement. Father would often have to go to jail. Because of the tense environment, my brothers and I were being sent to our mother's parents' house, to Shri Rajaji. On the way from Delhi to Madras, we stayed for a few days in Bombay with Amma and Appa. From Bombay, a family friend was going to take us to Madras. The thought of being so far away from my mother for so long made me sad and also cross with her; I was considering never speaking to Amma and Appa again – the easy, courageous thought of a young girl. There was the happiness of going to our mother's childhood home, but the idea of being sent there struck me as injustice.

Anyway, I was in a habit of often being cross with mother. So she thought of giving me a doll to bring me around. One afternoon, while Appa was busy with some national movement work, Amma went out to buy me a doll. And, from some shop in the big city of Bombay, she got me a very beautiful foreign-made one. My heart leaped with happiness as soon as I saw it. Still, I pretended to be cross with mother. Only the company of a lovely, beautiful doll could make up somewhat for mother's absence. But I stayed cross and pretended to be unaffected.

Today, fifty years later, I still regret not having hugged mother and not having expressed my joy at getting that doll. When mother tried to hug me, I jerked away and wrapped my arms around the doll instead. And, in that great vision of motherhood, I was being introduced to something. In those days, toys made in India could not be found in big city shops. The movement to resurrect rural industry and craft found itself crashing against the foreign rule. In the middle of the freedom movement and its abnormal routines and busyness and uncertainty, my mother had taken out some time to get me a doll.

She could only find a foreign doll, but why wouldn't a mother buy it? The shunning of foreign goods was only one part of her truth. Amidst the *satyagraha*, she also had a thought for her own doll who was, for a long and uncertain time, going to be separated from her mother against her wishes. Even meeting again could be difficult. So, for her doll, mother bought a doll. Its being foreign was beside the point, and the meaning of its being foreign had also become immaterial. Her daughter needed something to keep her strong during the separation from her mother.

I – my mother's doll – hugged my new doll.

Since then, whenever in life I was faced with obstacles, big or small, dolls have been a source of comfort to me. Girls love dolls. But for me this love, coming out of the mud-houses of childhood, encompassing the madness of youth, took on, in the solitude of old age, the meanings of all ages, and became a symbol for all creation. In this journey of life, that gesture of my mother's love kept comforting me in all its colours and shapes. I was my mother's doll. Now, when I give shape to Mother Nature, I create myself.

It's been almost twenty-five years since I was introduced to this creative inspiration. Now, when I open a bundle of old clothes and tatters, I see multiple shapes and forms emerging effortlessly.

The capital of Italy, the beloved enchanting city of Rome, which has a special place in the glorious culture and history of Europe, was where my husband was posted as an official in a UN organization. Both our kids were growing up there. Kids grow up and their clothes grow small. But living as I was among all that glory, who could I give the old clothes to? Torn clothes and broken utensils showed up the meaninglessness of meaningful riches. No *kabaadi* (buyer of discards) would come to the doorstep there. In India, the *kabaadi*, who bought the meaninglessness of our meaningfulness with hard cash, would come to our door himself. The *kabaadi* is, in a way, an incarnation of God who can give our meaninglessness some meaning. In recycling lies the secret to the eternal reinvention of nature.

This philosophy was, at that time, not an articulation of my conscious wisdom. Whether it existed in my unconscious nature, that too is not yet clear to me. But this much for sure is true, that there was the inspiration to give some shape to my meaninglessness. The search for meaning in the meaningless.

When scraps of cloth, colours and broken buttons, fused bulbs and useless locks and keys from the trash become priceless, then all the pieces start coming together to take their shape. I was astonished by their emerging personalities. I had always been enchanted by the look and colour of the *banjaarans*, nomadic women of Rajasthan and Gujarat, but the voice that rose unbidden with the colour, shape and look of my creations was also the unbidden voice of the *banjaarans* – the voice coming from the infinite reaches of the seashore of life.

Banjaarans are the waves of the entirety of exiles, of lives and lifetimes. My creations instead of being my own kept creating themselves, and I myself was recreated in the form of an onlooker.

Once, from the torn soiled scraps of cloth, a shape emerged that even I could not stand to look at – a representation of an unbearable tragic reality of our times. A torn *lehenga*, an aanchal of cloth and straw, a blouse with only one sleeve, uncombed and unwashed hair. No ornament on the hands, neck or ears. Not even holding a broom, which could have kept the figure safe and certain. In her hand, I had only kept a broken aluminum mug. 'No!' I said. 'How did this reality get created?' I opened up that shape and made it shapeless. That beggar woman of our reality today, giving company to her tattered clothes with her battered body – why did I find her misery accusatory? As if it were asking me: '*You* are the creator of my naked form. Then why does the shape of your creation cause your insides to scream?' But only by making the shape I had created shapeless, did I come to the realization. The shape of Mother Nature who is showing us the way by boiling rice for us even in broken aluminum pots... The wealth all around is of no use to her. Nature is free.

The Meaning of Swaraj

❧

The world today celebrates *satyagraha* – truth and non-violence as experienced, experimented and lived by Mohandas Karamchand Gandhi. I wonder if at any time in human history the philosophical and moral concepts of truth and compassion have been the subject of such collective and conscious celebrations throughout the world. Truth, courage and compassion continue to remain relevant and are, in fact, the desperate need of today.

The world today is also governed by fear because of things like environmental pollution, human violence and terrorism. Hence, we all seek an answer or a message that will allow us to realize the essence of compassion and of truth itself. The concept of *satyagraha* (the search for truth) is inseparable from fearlessness as Gandhi so often emphasized. Mahatma Gandhi inspired fearless love and trust in others.

Swaraj is the Sanskrit word for self-rule and liberty. Literally, it means control over one's self rather than simply independence from someone else's rule. To achieve *swaraj*, therefore, a society or a nation must display individual and collective responsibility and accountability.

The concept of *swaraj* was defined to me in an elementary but powerful way by my grandmother, Kasturba, when I was a child. It was before India became free. Bapu and Kasturba were both imprisoned in the Aga Khan Palace in Pune at the time. My parents had taken my brothers and me to visit them. Kasturba was lying in bed, very frail and ill, but she was very happy to see us. There was a huge room next to the section of the palace where Bapu, Kasturba and a few others had been detained. I wanted to go and play there. 'Ba,' I began to ask my grandmother, 'can I go and play in that room? There are no guards there; I can easily go and play there and come back.' 'Which room?' Ba asked. When I pointed to the room she said, 'No, my child. You should not go there. We should not go where we aren't permitted to go. We do not need a guard to keep a watch over us. We should be responsible.'

Kasturba died a few weeks later in the same prison, but only after teaching her granddaughter the meaning of self-control and responsibility – the essence of *swaraj*.

Extract from a speech by Tara Gandhi Bhattacharjee in 2010 at the Gandhi Smriti Memorial

Family Tree of Mahatma Gandhi

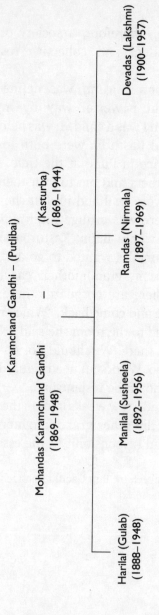

Karamchand Gandhi – (Putlibai)

|

Mohandas Karamchand Gandhi — (Kasturba)
(1869–1948)　　　　　　(1869–1944)

Harilal (Gulab)　　Manilal (Susheela)　　Ramdas (Nirmala)　　Devadas (Lakshmi)
(1888–1948)　　　(1892–1956)　　　　(1897–1969)　　　　(1900–1957)

Family Tree of Mahatma Gandhi

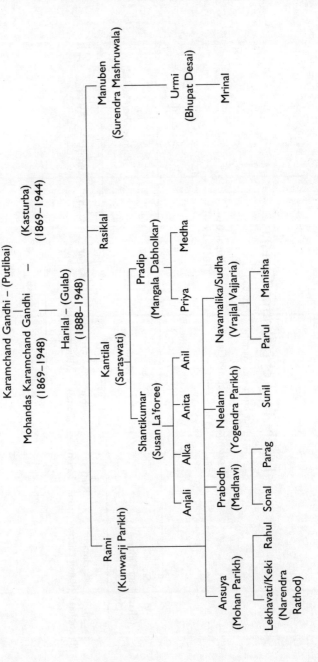

Family Tree of Mahatma Gandhi

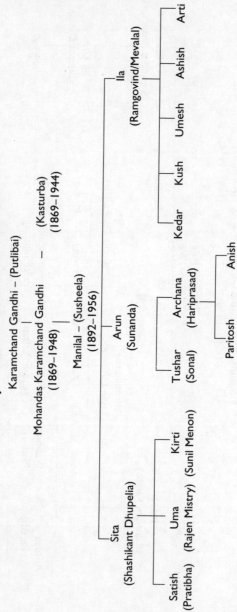

Family Tree of Mahatma Gandhi

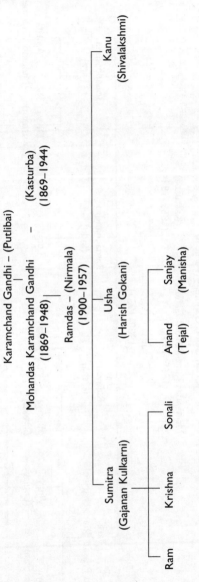

Karamchand Gandhi – (Putlibai)

Mohandas Karamchand Gandhi   –   (Kasturba)
(1869–1948)   (1869–1944)

Ramdas – (Nirmala)
(1900–1957)

Sumitra   Usha
(Gajanan Kulkarni)   (Harish Gokani)

Ram   Krishna   Sonali

Anand   Sanjay
(Tejal)   (Manisha)

Kanu
(Shivalakshmi)

Family Tree of Mahatma Gandhi

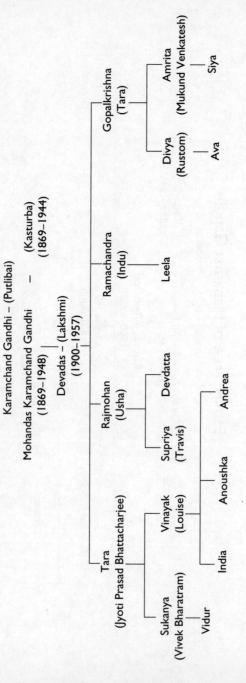

Karamchand Gandhi – (Putlibai)

Mohandas Karamchand Gandhi   –   (Kasturba)
(1869–1948)   (1869–1944)

Devadas – (Lakshmi)
(1900–1957)

Tara
(Jyoti Prasad Bhattacharjee)

Rajmohan
(Usha)

Ramachandra
(Indu)

Gopalkrishna
(Tara)

Sukanya
(Vivek Bharatram)

Vidur

Vinayak
(Louise)

India

Anoushka

Andrea

Supriya
(Travis)

Devdatta

Leela

Divya
(Rustom)

Ava

Amrita
(Mukund Venkatesh)

Siya

Glossary

PLACES

Bhatpara
A suburban town and municipality under the Barrackpore subdivision in North 24 Parganas district in the state of West Bengal.

Connaught Circus
One of the largest commercial centres in Delhi, it was developed as the central business district of Lutyens' Delhi.

Birla House
Originally the house of Indian business tycoons, the Birlas, where Mahatma Gandhi spent the last few months of his life and was assassinated on January 30 1948. It was acquired by the Government of India in 1971 to be turned into the Gandhi Smriti museum.

Hanuman Mandir
An ancient Hindu temple of the monkey-god in Connaught Place, New Delhi, it is claimed to be one of the five temples of Mahabharata days in Delhi.

Jama Masjid	Principal mosque of Old Delhi in India.
Aga Khan Palace	It was built in the year 1892 by Sultan Muhammed Shah, Aga Khan III in Pune as an act of charity for the poor drastically hit by famine. From 9 August 1942 to 6 May 1944, this palace was a prison for Mahatma Gandhi, Kasturba and his secretary Mahadev Bhai Desai. The latter two died during their captivity.
Porbandar	A coastal city in the Indian state of Gujarat, perhaps best known for being the birthplace of Mahatma Gandhi.
Sewagram	A place that Mahatma Gandhi made for community service. The ashram employed some Harijans (untouchables) in the common kitchen to break caste barrier.
Shimla	Capital city of the Indian state of Himachal Pradesh. In 1864, it was declared the summer capital of the British Raj in India.
Valmiki Ashram	A Harijan colony on Redding Road (now Mandir Marg) where Mahatma Gandhi spent some months in 1946.

PEOPLE

Manu and Abha	Mahatma Gandhi's grandnieces
Maulana Azad	Indian Muslim scholar and a senior political leader of the Indian independence movement. Following India's independence, he became the first Minister of Education in the Indian government.
Sarla Bhen	One of Mahatma Gandhi's English daughters. Her name originally was Catherine Mary Heilman. She went from village to village helping families of political prisoners.
Ghanshyam Das Birla	An Indian businessman and member of the influential Birla Family.
Sir Stafford Cripps	British Labour politician of the first half of the 20th century. In 1946, he returned to India as part of the Cabinet Mission, which proposed various formulae for independence to the Indian leaders.
Mahadev Bhai Desai	Indian independence activist and nationalist writer, he was also the personal secretary of Mahatma Gandhi.
Devadas Gandhi	Fourth and youngest son of Mohandas Gandhi, he participated actively in his father's movement, spending many terms in jail. He was also a prominent journalist, serving as editor of the *Hindustan Times*.

Harilal Gandhi	Eldest son of Mohandas and Kasturba Gandhi.
Manilal Gandhi	Second of the four sons of Mohandas Gandhi. In 1897, Manilal travelled to South Africa for the first time, where he spent time working at the Phoenix Ashram near Durban. After a brief visit to India in 1917, Manilal returned to South Africa to assist in printing the *Indian Opinion,* a Gujarati-English weekly at Phoenix, Durban. By 1918, Manilal was doing most of the work for the press and took over in 1920 as its editor.
Ramdas Gandhi	Third son of Mohandas Gandhi, he was active in his father's Indian independence movement.
Gopu/Gopalkrishna Gandhi	Youngest child and third son of Devadas and Lakshmi Gandhi.
Monu/Rajmohan Gandhi	Second child and first son of Devadas and Lakshmi Gandhi.
Ramu/Ramchandra Gandhi	Second son of Devadas and Lakshmi Gandhi. Indian philosopher.
Mohammed Ali Jinnah	20th century lawyer, politician and statesman who is known as the founder of Pakistan. He is popularly known in Pakistan as *Quaid-e-Azam*.
Susheela Kaki	Susheela Mashruwala. Wife of Manilal Gandhi.

Kasturba	Kasturba Gandhi.Wife of Mohandas Karamchand Gandhi.
Rajkumari Amrit Kaur	Freedom fighter from the Kapurthala princely family. She was the first Minister of Health in free India.
Badshah Khan	Khan Abdul Ghaffar Khan or Frontier Gandhi was a Pashtun political and spiritual leader known for his non-violent resistance to British Rule in India.
Lord and Lady Mountbatten	Lord Mountbatten was the last viceroy of India, with the charge of overseeing the transition of British India to independence. Lady Mountbatten was his wife, Edwina.
Sardar Patel	Indian barrister and statesman, one of the leaders of the Indian National Congress and one of the founding fathers of India. He was also known as the 'Iron Man of India'. In India and across the world, he was often addressed as Sardar, which means 'chief' in Hindi, Urdu and Persian.
Pandit Nehru/ Jawaharlal Nehru	Freedom fighter and the first prime minister of free India.
Rajaji/Anna/ C. Rajagopalachari	Freedom fighter, statesman, administrator, writer and scholar, the first governor general of India. Also the maternal grandfather of Tara Gandhi Bhattacharjee.

Satyajit Ray	Satyajit Ray (1921–1992) was an Indian Bengali filmmaker. He is regarded as one of the greatest auteurs of 20th century cinema.
Jamini Roy	Indian painter.
Lal Bahadur Shastri	Second prime minister of the Republic of India and a significant figure in the Indian independence movement.
MS Subbulakshmi	Renowned Carnatic Music exponent who was awarded the highest civilian honour in India, the Bharat Ratna, in 1988. She died in 2004.
Sumi	Daughter of Ramdas Gandhi.
Rabindranath Tagore	Indian Bengali polymath who reshaped his region's literature and music. Author of *Gitanjali,* he became the first non-European to win the Nobel Prize in Literature in 1913.

APPELLATIONS

Amma	mother
Anna	elder brother
Appa	father
Ba	grandmother (especially used in Gujarat and was used to address Kasturba Gandhi)
Bapu-ji	Mahatma Gandhi
Bhabi	sister-in-law/wife of elder brother

Dada	paternal grandfather
Dadi	paternal grandmother
Ji	an honorific
Kaka	paternal uncle
Mama	maternal uncle
Nana	maternal grandfather
Pandit	a learned man (was especially used for Jawaharlal Nehru)
Tau	paternal uncle/father's elder brother

OTHERS

Advaita	Advaita Vedanta is considered to be the most influential and most dominant sub-school of the Vedanta (literally, end or the goal of the *Vedas*) school of Hindu philosophy. Advaita (literally, non-duality) is a system of thought where 'Advaita' refers to the identity of the 'Self' (Atman) and the 'Whole' (Brahman).
Ahimsa	non-violence
Ashram	Traditionally, an ashram is a spiritual hermitage. Additionally, today the term ashram often denotes a locus of Indian cultural activity such as yoga, music study or religious instruction, the moral equivalent of a studio or dojo.
Basti	settlement

Bhajan	hymns
Brahmacharya	Brahmacharya is one of the four stages of life in an age-based social system as laid out in the *Manu Smriti* and later classical sanskrit texts in Hinduism. It refers to an educational period of 14–20 years, which starts before puberty. During this time the traditional Vedic sciences are studied, along with the religious texts contained within the *Vedas* and *Upanishads*. This stage of life is characterized by the practice of celibacy.
Brahmin	A name used to designate a member of one of the four *varnas* (castes) in the traditional Hindu society. Traditionally, Brahmins were those people who had attained the highest spiritual knowledge and who read the *Vedas*.
Charkha	spinning wheel
Dhoti	The dhoti, also known as *pancha* or *veshti* is the traditional men's garment in India, Bangladesh and Sri Lanka.
Diwali	festival of lights in India
Gandhi Smriti and Darshan Samiti	GSDS was formed in 1984 by the merger of Gandhi Darshan at Rajghat and Gandhi Smriti as an autonomous body. Gandhi Smriti, housed in the

Old Birla House on 5, Tees January Marg, New Delhi, is the sacred place where Mahatma Gandhi's epic life ended on 30 January 1948. Mahatma Gandhi had lived in this house from 9 September 1947 to 30 January 1948.

Garara	A traditional garment traditionally worn by North Indian muslim women in the Subcontinent. It consists of a short tunic, a dupatta (veil), and a pair of wide-legged pants ruched at the knees so they flare out dramatically.
Grihastha	Second phase of an individual's life in the Vedic ashram system. It is often called 'the householder's life' revolving as it does around the duties of maintaining a household and leading a family-centred life.
Harijan	Harijan was a term used by Mahatma Gandhi for Dalits. He said it was wrong to call people 'untouchable' and called them Harijans, which means children of God.
Hindustan Times	Leading Indian English-language newspaper
ICS	Indian Civil Service
Iyengar	Iyengar or Ayyangar is a caste given to Hindu Brahmins of Tamil origin who follow the Visishtadvaita philosophy propounded by Sri Ramanujacharya.

Iyer	Title given to the caste of Hindu Brahmin communities of Tamil origin. Most Iyers are followers of the Advaita philosophy propounded by Adi Shankara.
Salwar-kameez	Traditional dress worn by women in South Asia and Central Asia. Salwar are loose pajama-like trousers. The legs are wide at the top and narrow at the ankle. The kameez is a long shirt or tunic.
Lehenga	A costume of worn by women in Central and North India.
Kasturba Gandhi National Memorial Trust	Established in 1945 by Mahatma Gandhi to address the issues of women in rural India, it has its headquarters in Kasturbagram (Indore) and 22 state branches all over the country.
Kayastha	A caste of Hindus in India whose traditional role was that of record-keeping for and administrating the state
Khadi	Indian cloth made out of threads spun on the *charkha*
Lota	A small spherical brass or copper vessel used to hold water or milk
Mantra	Chants that originated in the Vedic tradition of India
Pathans	Ethnic Afghans

Ramdhun	Popular devotional song (*Raghupati Raghav Raja Ram…*) that was a favourite of Mahatma Gandhi's
Sadhvi	Female ascetic
Sanyasa	The order of life of the renouncer within the Hindu scheme of ashramas
Satyagraha	Non-violent resistance
Shloka	The basis for Indian epic verse, occurring more frequently than any other meter in classical Sanskrit poetry
Swaraj	Self-governance or self-rule
Tonga	Horse carriage
Vanaprastha	The stage of life in the Vedic ashram system in which a person gradually withdraws from the world
Visvabharati University at Shantiniketan	A central university for research and teaching at Shantiniketan in West Bengal, founded by Rabindranath Tagore